101 WRITING PROMPTS FOR KIDS

STORY STARTERS TO SPARK CREATIVITY - FOR KIDS 8 TO 12

JEFFREY C. CHAPMAN

MEDIALUSION GROUP

CONTENTS

INTRODUCTION

Hello and welcome to "101 Writing Prompts for Kids," a wonderful collection of story ideas for you to explore your creativity and imagination. The only thing that limits this book is your imagination. It's more than just a list of writing tasks.

There are 101 carefully thought-out writing ideas inside that cover a wide range of topics, from fantasy to adventure to mystery and more. Each prompt is an idea for where to begin, a way to spark your mind and keep your creative engine going. Through these pages, you'll find talking animals, magical countries, adventures that take you back in time, and a lot more.

"101 Writing Prompts for Kids" isn't just about getting kids to be creative, though. It's also about getting better at writing, learning new words, and getting the courage to share your own stories. This book is an ode to creativity, a play area for kids' thoughts, and proof of the power of words. So get your pen, computer or tablet, clear your mind, and get ready for a creative writing journey you'll never forget

PLEASE CONSIDER LEAVING A REVIEW

Hello there!

As an author, I know just how important reviews are for getting the word out about my work. When readers leave a review on Amazon or any other book stores, it helps others discover my book and decide whether it's right for them.

Plus, it gives me valuable feedback on what readers enjoyed and what they didn't.

So if you've read my book and enjoyed it, I would really appreciate it if you took a moment to leave a review on Amazon. It doesn't have to be long or complicated - just a few words about what you thought of the book would be incredibly helpful.

Thank you so much for your support!

Jeff

CHAPTER 1

THE SILENT FOREST

Prompt:
Imagine a forest where animals communicate without talking. How do
they interact, and what secrets do you learn from observing them?

To Get You Started:

In Silent Forest, the animals communicate as well, but not through sound. Wonder and take a closer look in how the animals of Silent Forest communicates with their unique ways. How do they find each other? They could use gestures, change in color and so on. Perhaps they use smells or even make patterns on the ground to communicate. Describe different ways of silent communication that you have and draw from how animals relate with each other. What secrets about their lives and lifestyles - and the ecosystem - are you unearthing? What does this silence between species teach you in terms of understanding and empathy? This prompt invites you to explore a world where communication takes on a whole new form, full of subtlety and beauty.

Questions to Help You Make it Even Better:

1. How do these silent forms of communication change your perspective on how animals interact?

2. What challenges do the animals face in communicating this way, and how do they overcome them?

3. If you could learn one of these silent communication methods, which one would it be and why?

Optional Activity:

Create an illustration or a series of pictures showing different animals in the Silent Forest and their unique ways of communicating. Include captions explaining each method of communication.

Chapter 2

A Day as an Animal

Prompt:
Choose an animal and write about a day in its life from its perspective.

To Get You Started:

In this exercise, you get to step into the paws, fins, or wings of an animal of your choice. Imagine what it would be like to live as that animal for a day. What would you see, hear, or do? Think about the animal's habitat, its daily activities, and how it interacts with other animals. If you're a bird, describe soaring through the sky. If you're a fish, explain what the underwater world looks like.

Questions to Help You Make it Even Better:

1. If you were a creature that only comes out at night, like an owl, what would your nighttime adventures be like? Let's talk about what you can see and hear when it's dark outside!

2. Imagine how your day would change if you were a teeny tiny creature, like a little mouse, instead of a big and mighty elephant. It would be quite an adventure, don't you think?

3. Imagine a cool animal that loves hanging out with its friends, just like a penguin! How do you make friends and talk to people in your neighborhood?

Optional Activity:

Create an Animal Journal. Imagine a day in the life of your chosen animal, and write a diary entry from its perspective. Include details about where it lives, what it eats, how it interacts with other animals, and any adventures it might have in its natural habitat. You can also draw illustrations to accompany the diary entry, showing the animal in various activities throughout its day, such as foraging for food, playing, or resting. This activity will help you dive deeper into the animal's world, encouraging empathy and understanding for its lifestyle and environment.

CHAPTER 3

THE LOST DRAGON EGG

Prompt:
You find a dragon egg. Describe how you care for it and what happens
when it hatches.

To Get You Started:

Imagine finding a mysterious, shimmering dragon egg. What does it look like? Is it large, small, colorful, or perhaps glowing? Think about how you would take care of this magical egg. Would you keep it warm, read stories to it, or play music? And the most exciting part: what happens when the dragon hatches? Describe the dragon and your first interaction with it. Is it friendly, mischievous, or shy?

Questions to Help You Make it Even Better:

1. What kind of magical abilities would your dragon have? Can it breathe fire, create ice, or perhaps become invisible?

2. How would you communicate with your dragon? Would you understand each other's language, or would you find another way to communicate?

3. If the dragon grows too big for your home, where would you go to find it a new home? Would it be a mountain, a forest, or somewhere else entirely?

Optional Activity:

Draw a picture of your dragon egg and the dragon that hatches from it. Use your imagination to add unique colors and features.

CHAPTER 4

A DAY WITH DINOSAURS

Prompt:
Travel back in time to when dinosaurs roamed the Earth. What do you
see and learn?

To Get You Started:

Imagine stepping into a time machine and going back millions of years to the age of the dinosaurs. As you explore this ancient world, describe the dinosaurs and other prehistoric creatures you see. What are their sizes, colors, and behaviors? Observe the environment around you - the plants, the landscape, and the sky. How is it different from the world you know? What exciting discoveries do you make about these magnificent creatures and their habitat?

Questions to Help You Make it Even Better:

1. If you could follow a herd of herbivore dinosaurs, like Triceratops or Stegosaurus, what might you learn about their daily life?

2. What would you do if you saw a dinosaur hunting for its food? How would you stay safe while observing?

3. Imagine you found a fossil during your adventure. What kind of fossil is it and what does it tell you about the dinosaur it came from?

Optional Activity:
Create a dinosaur journal. Draw pictures of the dinosaurs you 'meet' and write down interesting facts about each one, like what they eat and how they might have behaved.

CHAPTER 5

THE HIDDEN VILLAGE

Prompt:
You stumble upon a hidden village with an unusual culture. Tell the story
of your visit.

To Get You Started:

I MAGINE FINDING A SECRET village that's not on any map. This village has its own unique culture, traditions, and maybe even its own language or unusual technology. As you walk through the village, describe what you see, hear, and feel. How do the houses look? What kind of clothes do the villagers wear? Attend their festivals, taste their food, and participate in their daily activities. Share your experiences of learning about their way of life and what makes it special or different from your own.

Clarifying Questions:

1. How do the villagers react to your arrival? Are they welcoming, curious, or cautious?

2. What is the most surprising or interesting thing you learn about the village's culture or traditions?

3. If you could bring one aspect of the village's culture back to your own life, what would it be and why?

Optional Activity:
Create a map of the hidden village. Include key locations like houses, a town square, and any special landmarks. Label each part with a brief description.

CHAPTER 6

THE TALKING TREE

Prompt:
You find a tree that can talk and tell stories. What stories does it tell?

To Get You Started:

I MAGINE DISCOVERING A TREE that can speak and share stories from its long life. As you sit under its branches, the tree begins to recount tales from different times and places. What kind of stories does it tell? Maybe it shares memories of the wildlife that has lived among its branches, or tales of the people who have rested in its shade. Perhaps it tells of changes in the environment or secrets of the forest that only a tree would know.

Clarifying Questions:

1. If the tree could tell a story from before you were born, what era would it be from and what would the story be about?

2. How does the tree feel about the changes it has seen over the years, like the growth of a nearby city or the changing climate?

3. What advice or wisdom does the tree share with you based on its years of experience?

Optional Activity:

Write a short story or a poem from the perspective of the talking tree. Include details about its age, the things it has seen, and the wisdom it has to share.

Chapter 7

PIRATE ADVENTURE ON THE HIGH SEAS

Prompt:
You're a pirate searching for treasure. Describe your adventures.

To Get You Started:

I MAGINE YOU'RE A DARING pirate sailing across the vast oceans in search of hidden treasure. Think about your pirate ship, your loyal crew, and the map that guides you. What challenges do you face on your journey? Maybe you encounter stormy seas, mysterious islands, or other pirates! Describe the treasure you're seeking – is it gold, jewels, or something more unusual? Share the exciting moments and the clever ways you overcome obstacles in your quest.

Clarifying Questions:

1. What unique feature does your pirate ship have? Maybe it's incredibly fast, can turn invisible, or even fly!

2. Who is your most trusted crew member and why? Describe how they help you on your journey.

3. If you find the treasure, what do you plan to do with it? Will you share it, use it to go on more adventures, or maybe hide it again for others to find?

Optional Activity:

Draw a treasure map that leads to where you imagine the hidden treasure is located. Include landmarks, obstacles, and clues along the way.

CHAPTER 8

THE LIFE OF A SUPER-VILLAIN

Prompt:
Write a story from the perspective of a super-villain. What is their goal?

To Get You Started:

I MAGINE STEPPING INTO THE shoes of a super-villain. What makes them a villain? Think about their background, what led them to become a villain, and what their ultimate goal is. Is it world domination, revenge, or something more complex? Describe their secret lair, their extraordinary abilities or gadgets, and their plans for achieving their goal. Also, consider their encounters with superheroes or other characters. Does their goal change over time? How do they feel about being a villain?

Clarifying Questions:

1. What is your super-villain's weakness or vulnerability? How do they deal with this weakness?

2. How does your super-villain interact with their minions or allies? Are they a lone wolf or do they have a team?

3. If your super-villain had the chance to change their path, would they? What might prompt this change of heart?

Optional Activity:

Create a comic strip showing a key moment in your super-villain's life. This could be the moment they became evil, a confrontation with a hero, or a moment of self-reflection.

CHAPTER 9

THE WISHING WELL

Prompt:
You find a well that grants wishes. What do you wish for and what are
the consequences?

To Get You Started:

I MAGINE DISCOVERING A MAGICAL well that can make any wish come true. Think about what you would wish for. It could be something personal, like being the best at a sport or having a superpower, or something big, like world peace or endless candy! However, every wish comes with consequences. Describe what happens after your wish is granted. Does everything go as planned, or are there unexpected outcomes? This prompt encourages you to think about the responsibilities that come with power and the idea that sometimes what we wish for might not be what we really need or want.

Clarifying Questions:

1. How do you find the wishing well, and what makes you decide to trust it?

2. Before making a wish, do you consider asking others for their opinions or wishes, or do you make a wish solely based on what you want?

3. After seeing the consequences of your first wish, would you ever consider using the well again? What would you do differently?

Optional Activity:

Write a diary entry or a letter from the perspective of someone affected by your wish. How do they feel about the changes brought by your wish?

CHAPTER 10

THE BUTTERFLY WHO COULD TALK

Prompt:
You become friends with a talking butterfly and it shares secrets of the
natural world. What do you learn?

To Get You Started:

I N THIS ENCHANTING STORY, you become friends with a magical talking butterfly. This butterfly is not only a delightful companion but also a wise guide to the secrets of nature. As you spend time together, the butterfly shares fascinating insights about the environment, other animals, and plants. What does it reveal about the process of metamorphosis, the way flowers grow, or how other creatures communicate? This prompt encourages you to imagine the wonders of the natural world through the eyes of one of its smallest inhabitants.

Clarifying Questions:

1. What surprising fact does the butterfly reveal about how it sees the world with its compound eyes?

2. How does the butterfly describe its transformation from a caterpillar to its current form?

3. What advice does the butterfly give you about taking care of the environment?

Optional Activity:

Draw a picture of your adventures with the talking butterfly. Include the different animals and plants you learn about and label them with fun facts the butterfly taught you.

CHAPTER 11

THE WORLD'S BIGGEST PLAYGROUND

Prompt:
Imagine the most amazing playground. What does it have and what adventures do you have there?

To Get You Started:

P ICTURE YOURSELF STEPPING INTO the world's biggest and most incredible play-ground. This isn't just any ordinary playground – it's a wonderland of fun and adventure. Think about the different types of equipment and areas it might have. Are there sky-high slides, a maze of tunnels, or a castle with secret passages? Maybe there's a section that's like a mini city or a jungle gym that reaches into the clouds. Describe the adventures you have in this playground. Do you meet new friends, embark on imaginary quests, or discover hidden treasures?

Clarifying Questions:

1. If you could design one unique feature for this playground, what would it be and why?

2. How does playing in this playground make you feel? Do you feel like an explorer, a superhero, or something else?

3. What's the most challenging part of the playground, and how do you conquer it?

Optional Activity:

Draw a map of your dream playground. Include all the different areas and features you imagine, and give each one a creative name.

CHAPTER 12

THE PET DINOSAUR

Prompt:
You have a pet dinosaur. Describe your daily life and the fun challenges
you face.

To Get You Started:

I MAGINE HAVING A DINOSAUR as a pet in modern times! Think about what kind of dinosaur it is – a tiny, playful Velociraptor, a gentle giant like Brachiosaurus, or maybe a Triceratops with a personality as big as its horns. What is your daily routine with your dinosaur? Maybe you have to figure out what to feed it, how to play with it, or where it sleeps. Describe the hilarious and unexpected situations you find yourself in. How do you take your dinosaur for walks? What happens when it's bath time? This prompt encourages you to think creatively about caring for an unusual pet and the fun and challenges that come with it.

Clarifying Questions:

1. How do your friends and neighbors react to your pet dinosaur? Are they surprised, scared, or excited?

2. What's the biggest challenge you face in keeping a pet dinosaur, and how do you solve it?

3. If you could teach your dinosaur a trick, what would it be and why?

Optional Activity:

Draw a picture of you and your pet dinosaur doing your favorite activity together. Is it playing at the park, going for a swim, or something else entirely?

CHAPTER 13

THE ANIMAL WHISPERER

Prompt:
You discover that you can talk to animals. What conversations do you have
and what secrets do you learn?

To Get You Started:

I MAGINE ONE DAY YOU wake up and find out you have the incredible ability to talk to animals. What is the first animal you speak to, and what do you talk about? It could be a bird sharing the secrets of flight, a cat revealing the mysteries of its nine lives, or a dog discussing its keen sense of smell. Think about the different animals you might communicate with – both wild and domestic. What unique perspectives do they offer on life? How do they view humans? What do they think about their own lives in the wild or in homes? This prompt encourages you to explore the wonders of the animal kingdom from a unique and personal perspective.

Clarifying Questions:

1. How do the animals react when they realize you can understand them? Are they surprised, excited, or cautious?

2. What surprising or unexpected things do you learn from talking to different animals?

3. Is there an animal whose perspective changes how you see the world or your relationship with nature?

Optional Activity:

Write a short story or a diary entry about an extraordinary day spent conversing with various animals. Describe each animal's personality and the most interesting part of your conversation with them.

CHAPTER 14

THE SECRET UNDERWATER CITY

Prompt:
You find a hidden city under the sea. What is life like there, and what mysteries do you uncover?

To Get You Started:

I MAGINE DIVING DEEP INTO the ocean and discovering a secret city hidden beneath the waves. What does this underwater city look like? Are the buildings made of coral and shells, or do they have some advanced technology that's completely new to you? Explore the streets and meet its inhabitants – are they humans adapted to underwater life, mysterious sea creatures, or maybe a combination of both? Describe your day-to-day experiences in this city. What do you eat, where do you sleep, and how do you communicate with the locals? Share the mysteries and wonders you uncover. Perhaps there's a hidden treasure, an ancient prophecy, or a technological marvel that keeps the city hidden.

Clarifying Questions:

1. How did the city come to be under the sea? Was it always there, or was it submerged due to some event?

2. What challenges do you face living underwater, and how do you overcome them?

3. If you could bring one aspect of the underwater city back to the surface world, what would it be and why?

Optional Activity:

Draw a map or a detailed picture of the underwater city, including key locations and interesting features you discover on your adventures.

CHAPTER 15

THE TALKING VEHICLE

Prompt:
Your car, bike, or skateboard starts talking to you. What stories does it tell and where does it take you?

To Get You Started:

I MAGINE ONE DAY YOUR favorite mode of transportation – whether it's a family car, a bike, or even a skateboard – suddenly gains the ability to talk. What is the first thing it says to you? Think about the stories it might share. Maybe your car talks about the places it's been before it came to you, or your bike reminisces about the adventures it's seen with other riders. Perhaps your skateboard shares its dreams of performing the perfect trick. Describe the adventures and journeys you embark on together. Does your talking vehicle take you to hidden places in your city, secret paths in the forest, or even on a magical, flying ride?

Clarifying Questions:

1. How does having a talking vehicle change your daily routine or the way you view transportation?

2. What lessons or new skills do you learn from your adventures with your talking vehicle?

3. If you could go on a long journey with your vehicle, where would you go and why?

Optional Activity:

Write a travel diary entry or create a comic strip about an extraordinary day spent with your talking vehicle, detailing the places you visit and the conversations you have.

CHAPTER 16

THE ANCIENT TROLL PARK

Prompt:
You visit a park where Trolls exist. Describe your encounters and experiences.

To Get You Started:

I MAGINE VENTURING INTO A mysterious park known for its ancient troll inhabitants. These trolls might be different from what you've heard in stories; they could be wise, playful, or even a bit mischievous. As you walk through the park, describe the environment – is it a deep forest, a mountainous area, or something else? What do the trolls look like? Do they live in caves, under bridges, or in treehouses? Share your interactions with them. Perhaps you help a troll solve a problem, play a game of riddles, or learn about the park's magical secrets from them. This prompt encourages you to explore themes of myth, fantasy, and unexpected friendships.

Clarifying Questions:

1. How do you communicate with the trolls? Do they speak your language, or do you find another way to understand each other?

2. What's the most surprising thing you learn about the trolls and their way of life?

3. If you could bring something back from the troll park to remember your adventure, what would it be?

Optional Activity:

Draw a map of the Ancient Troll Park, including places where you met different trolls, obstacles you encountered, and any special landmarks.

CHAPTER 17

THE LAND WHERE KIDS MAKE THE RULES

Prompt:
Imagine a land where kids make all the rules. What rules would you create?

To Get You Started:

IN THIS EXCITING WORLD, children are in charge and they get to decide the rules for everything. Think about the rules you would make if you had this power. Would you have rules about bedtime, types of food, or how much time you spend playing? Maybe you would create rules for adults or invent new games and holidays. Consider not only the fun and freedom that come with creating rules but also the responsibility of making sure they are fair and keep everyone happy and safe. This prompt encourages you to think about leadership, fairness, and the consequences of rules.

Clarifying Questions:

1. How do you make sure that your rules are fair and consider everyone's needs and preferences?

2. What kind of system would you put in place to review and change rules if they're not working?

3. If there's a disagreement among kids about a rule, how would you resolve it?

Optional Activity:

Write a list of your top 10 rules for this land and explain why you chose each one. Then, draw a picture of what a typical day might look like in a place with these rules.

CHAPTER 18

THE WORLD'S GREATEST INVENTOR

Prompt:
You become the world's greatest inventor. What inventions do you create?

To Get You Started:

I MAGINE YOURSELF AS THE world's most renowned inventor, capable of creating things that can change the world. Think about the kinds of inventions you would like to bring to life. Would they be gadgets that make everyday life easier, machines that help protect the environment, or even fantastical devices that seem straight out of a science fiction story? Consider how your inventions would impact people's lives and the planet. This prompt invites you to explore your creativity, problem-solving skills, and vision for a better future.

Clarifying Questions:

1. How do your inventions reflect what you like and are passionate about? What inspired you to create them?

2. What challenges do you face in creating your inventions, and how do you overcome them?

3. How do you make sure that your inventions are used for good and benefit as many people as possible?

Optional Activity:

Draw a blueprint or a sketch of one of your inventions. Label the parts and write a short description of how it works and its benefits.

CHAPTER 19

THE MUSIC THAT CHANGES THE WORLD

Prompt:
You find a musical instrument that can change the world around you.
How do you use it?

To Get You Started:

I MAGINE DISCOVERING A MUSICAL instrument with the extraordinary power to change the world. Each note you play could create something new or alter something existing. Think about what kind of instrument it is – a flute, a guitar, a piano, or something entirely unique. What changes do you create with your music? Do you bring happiness and peace, heal the sick, or maybe grow lush forests and clean the oceans? Also, consider the responsibilities that come with such a powerful instrument. How do you decide when and how to use it? This prompt invites you to explore the power of music and its impact on the world, as well as themes of responsibility and ethical decision-making.

Clarifying Questions:

1. How does playing the instrument make you feel? Do you feel powerful, overwhelmed, or hopeful?

2. What challenges or dilemmas do you face in deciding how to use the instrument's power?

3. How do others react to the changes you create with the music? Are they supportive, fearful, or something else?

Optional Activity:

Write a poem about a day you spent with the instrument, focusing on a specific change you created and its effects on the world around you.

CHAPTER 20

THE ENCHANTED PLAYROOM

Prompt:
In the Enchanted Playroom, your toys come to life at night with magical abilities. What adventures do they have?

To Get You Started:

I MAGINE A WORLD WHERE, once the clock strikes midnight, your playroom trans- forms into an enchanted realm where all your toys gain magical abilities and unique personalities. Each toy has its own special power – maybe the teddy bear can speak to animals, the action figures become super-strong, or the dolls can cast spells.

Think about the adventures your toys embark on in the Enchanted Playroom. Do they protect the playroom from imaginary villains, go on quests to find hidden treasures within the room, or create magical worlds where they have fantastic adventures? Consider the relationships between your toys. Are there leaders and heroes, loyal companions, or even mischievous pranksters?

Think of the challenges they face in their nightly adventures. Maybe they work together to fix a broken toy, solve the mystery of a missing puzzle piece, or navigate the obstacles of a suddenly vast and unfamiliar room.

As the sun rises and the magic fades, the toys return to their usual places. What evidence do they leave behind of their nighttime adventures, and how do you imagine their stories based on these clues?

Clarifying Questions:

1. What magical ability would you like each of your favorite toys to have?

2. If you could join your toys in one of their nightly adventures, what would it be?

3. How do the toys' adventures reflect their personalities or the games you play with them during the day?

Optional Activity:

Create a 'Nightly Adventure Log' where you write and illustrate stories about the magical adventures your toys have at night. Each story can focus on a different toy or group of toys and their unique escapades in the Enchanted Playroom.

CHAPTER 21

MAGICAL SCHOOL ADVENTURE

Prompt:
Write about a day at a school where everyone has a unique magical power.
What is your power and how do you use it?

To Get You Started:

I MAGINE ATTENDING A SCHOOL where each student and teacher has a unique magical power. What would your magical power be? It could be anything from controlling elements like fire or water, to shape-shifting, time manipulation, or telepathy. Describe a typical day at this magical school. How do you use your power in classes? Are there special subjects taught based on different powers? Also, think about how students interact – do they help each other, compete, or even play magical pranks? Consider the challenges and adventures you face, whether it's mastering your power, dealing with magical mishaps, or embarking on spellbinding quests.

Clarifying Questions:

1. How did you discover your magical power, and how do you feel about it?

2. What are the most exciting and the most challenging aspects of having your power?

3. If you could swap powers with a friend for a day, which power would you choose and why?

Optional Activity:

Create a diary entry detailing an extraordinary event at your magical school, focusing on how you and your friends use your powers to overcome it.

CHAPTER 22

TIME TRAVEL TRIP

Prompt:
Imagine you have a time machine. Where and when would you go? Describe your adventures.

To Get You Started:

P ICTURE YOURSELF WITH THE incredible ability to travel through time. With a time machine, every era of history and the future is within your reach. Where is your first destination? Perhaps you want to witness a significant historical event, like the building of the Pyramids or the first moon landing. Maybe you're curious to see a glimpse of the future. As you journey through different times, describe the sights, sounds, and people you encounter. How do the clothes, technology, and buildings change? What kind of interactions do you have with the people or creatures you meet? Think about the lessons you learn from these travels and how they shape your understanding of the world. Remember to consider how you navigate the challenges of time travel, like fitting into different eras or ensuring you don't alter the course of history.

Clarifying Questions:

1. What made you to choose the specific times and places you visited?

2. How do you ensure that you blend in and don't disrupt the timeline during your travels?

3. If you could meet any historical figure or future leader, who would it be and why?

Optional Activity:

Create a time traveler's diary. For each destination, write a diary entry describing your experiences, the historical or futuristic setting, and any interesting characters you meet.

CHAPTER 23

SPACE EXPLORER

Prompt:
You're an astronaut exploring a new planet. What does it look like and
what creatures do you find?

To Get You Started:

A S A BRAVE ASTRONAUT, you've landed on an unknown planet far away in the galaxy. Describe what this new world looks like. What color is the sky? What kind of landscapes does it have – mountains, oceans, forests, or something entirely different? As you explore, talk about the alien creatures or plants you discover. Are they friendly, shy, or something else? How do they look and behave? Maybe you find a creature that can change colors or a plant that sings when the sun rises. Think about how you document your discoveries and what you do to ensure both your safety and the protection of the alien environment. This prompt invites you to let your imagination run wild with ideas of extraterrestrial life and unknown worlds.

Clarifying Questions:

1. How do you prepare for your exploration, and what tools do you use to study the planet and its inhabitants?

2. What's the most surprising or unexpected thing you discover on this planet?

3. If you could bring back one thing from the planet to Earth for further study, what would it be?

Optional Activity:
Create a space explorer's journal with drawings and descriptions of the new creatures and plants you find on the planet. Include notes on their habits and how they interact with their environment.

CHAPTER 24

UNDERWATER WORLD

Prompt:
Describe a city under the sea. Who lives there and what are their daily
activities?

To Get You Started:

D IVE INTO THE DEPTHS of the ocean to discover a bustling underwater city. What does this city look like? Are the buildings made of coral and shells, or do they have some advanced technology that's uniquely adapted to underwater life? Think about the inhabitants of this city. Are they humans who have adapted to live underwater, merpeople, or a completely new species? Describe their appearance, culture, and way of life. What are their daily activities – do they go to school, have jobs, or participate in underwater sports or arts? Also, consider how they interact with the marine environment and wildlife. This prompt invites you to explore a world where the ocean's mysteries are a part of everyday life.

Clarifying Questions:

1. How do the residents of this underwater city travel from one place to another?

2. What kind of technology or magic do they use to make life under the sea possible?

3. What unique challenges do they face living underwater, and how do they over-come them?

Optional Activity:

Draw a detailed map or a series of pictures of the underwater city, highlighting key locations like homes, schools, and special landmarks.

CHAPTER 25

LOST IN A FANTASY FOREST

Prompt:
Describe a forest filled with mythical creatures. What adventures do you
have there?

To Get You Started:

I MAGINE YOURSELF WANDERING INTO a forest unlike any other, a place where the trees are ancient and the air is filled with enchantment. This forest is home to a myriad of mythical creatures. Describe the creatures you encounter – are there unicorns grazing in meadows, fairies flitting between flowers, or perhaps talking animals with wise advice? What does the forest look like? Maybe there are trees with leaves of shimmering silver or streams that sparkle with magic. Think about the adventures and challenges you face in this forest. Do you help a creature in need, uncover a hidden treasure, or solve an ancient riddle? This prompt invites you to explore a world of wonder, danger, and mystery, where every step could lead to a new discovery.

Clarifying Questions:

1. How do you navigate and find your way in this mystical forest?

2. What unique characteristics or abilities do the mythical creatures have?

3. If you could take a souvenir back from the fantasy forest, what would it be and why?

Optional Activity:

Draw a map of the fantasy forest, marking the locations of different creatures and significant landmarks you encounter on your adventure.

CHAPTER 26

THE DREAM JOURNAL

Prompt:

Write about a dream you had. Was it a fantasy, a nightmare, or something else?

To Get You Started:

I MAGINE GOING DEEP INTO your own dream journal to describe a dream you recently had. Dreams can be fantastical, frightening, mysterious, or even funny. What did you dream about? Was it a grand adventure in a magical kingdom, a spooky encounter in a haunted house, or a bizarre series of events that made little sense? Describe the setting of your dream, the characters you met, and the feelings you experienced. Think about the strange and wonderful things that can happen in dreams, like flying, meeting talking animals, or discovering hidden abilities. Also, consider if there was a message or a lesson in your dream. Sometimes, dreams can be a way of processing your thoughts and feelings about real life.

Clarifying Questions:

1. How did the dream start and end? Did it have a clear storyline, or was it more abstract?

2. What emotions did you feel during the dream, and did they change as the dream progressed?

3. Did anything in the dream relate to your real life, such as a person you know, a place you've been, or a situation you've experienced?

Optional Activity:

Create a dream diary entry with illustrations. Draw the most vivid scenes or characters from your dream and write captions explaining their significance.

CHAPTER 27

THE INVISIBLE KID

Prompt:
Write a story about a day in the life of a kid who becomes invisible.

To Get You Started:

I MAGINE WAKING UP ONE morning to discover that you have become invisible! How does your day unfold? Think about the adventures and challenges you would face. What would be the first thing you do after realizing you're invisible? Maybe you play harmless pranks, eavesdrop on conversations, or embark on a secret mission. How do people around you react to your sudden disappearance? Consider both the fun aspects and the difficulties of being unseen. Does your invisibility have a time limit, or can you control it? Also, think about what you learn from this experience. Does being invisible give you a new perspective on the world and the people around you?

Clarifying Questions:

1. What are some unexpected problems you encounter while being invisible?

2. How do you communicate with others when they can't see you?

3. What would you do if you had the chance to be invisible for just one more day?

Optional Activity:

Create a comic strip showing a key event in the day of the invisible kid. Illustrate the challenges, the funny moments, and the reactions of those around them.

CHAPTER 28

THE MAGIC PAINTBRUSH

Prompt:
Everything you paint becomes real. What do you create?

To Get You Started:

I MAGINE HAVING A PAINTBRUSH with the power to bring anything you paint to life. What would you choose to paint? Think about the possibilities – you could paint animals that become your pets, landscapes you could step into, or even imaginary creatures that have never been seen before. Consider how you use this power. Do you create things for fun, to help others, or to solve problems? Maybe you paint a tree that grows money or a meal that feeds the hungry. Also, think about the responsibilities that come with such a magical tool. How do you make sure your creations are safe and positive for the world around you?

Clarifying Questions:

1. How do you decide what to paint? What inspires your creations?

2. What challenges do you encounter with the things you bring to life?

3. If you could share your magic paintbrush with someone else for a day, who would it be and why?

Optional Activity:

Draw a picture of one of your magical paintbrush creations. Write a short story or description about how you created it and what it does.

CHAPTER 29

A JOURNEY THROUGH A BOOK

Prompt:
You can enter any book you want. Which book do you choose and what happens?

To Get You Started:

I MAGINE HAVING THE MAGICAL ability to step inside any book and become part of its story. Which book would you choose to enter? Would you dive into a tale of adventure and exploration, a fantasy world filled with magic and mythical creatures, or maybe a historical novel to experience a different time period? Describe your journey inside the book. How do you interact with the characters and the world around you? Do you follow the story as it's written, or do your actions create new twists and turns? Think about the challenges you face in the book's world and how being part of the story changes your perspective on it. Also, consider what lessons you learn from this unique experience.

Clarifying Questions:

1. How do you feel when you first enter the book's world, and how do your feelings change throughout your adventure?

2. What role do you take on in the story – are you a hero, a sidekick, or a completely new character?

3. If you could bring something or someone back from the book's world into your own, what or who would it be?

Optional Activity:

Create a scrapbook page or a diary entry about your journey in the book. Include drawings or descriptions of the characters you meet and the places you visit.

CHAPTER 30

THE LAND OF SWEETS

Prompt:
Describe a land made entirely of candy and sweets. What adventures do
you have there?

To Get You Started:

IMAGINE A MAGICAL LAND where everything is made of candy and sweets. The trees are made of licorice, the houses are gingerbread, rivers flow with chocolate, and the mountains are scoops of ice cream. What does this sweet world look like, smell like, and, most importantly, taste like? Explore this delectable land and describe your adventures. Perhaps you help the marshmallow people solve a mystery, join a race against the gummy bears, or embark on a quest to find a legendary candy hidden in a sugar castle. Think about the challenges you might face – maybe a chocolate lake melting in the sun or a sticky candy forest. This prompt invites you to dive into a world of imagination and sweetness.

Clarifying Questions:

1. How do you travel around in this land of sweets? Do you ride on a peppermint stick boat, take a bubble gum balloon, or something else?

2. What kind of sweet treats do you encounter, and which is your favorite?

3. If you could bring one of the sweet creations back to the real world, what would it be?

Optional Activity:

Draw a map of the Land of Sweets, labeling different areas like the Chocolate Chasm, the Gummy Bear Garden, or the Lollipop Woods.

CHAPTER 31

THE GIANT GARDEN

Prompt:
Imagine you're tiny and exploring a garden full of giant plants and insects. What do you discover?

To Get You Started:

P ICTURE YOURSELF SHRUNK DOWN to the size of an ant, exploring a garden where everything is enormous compared to you. The blades of grass tower like skyscrapers, flowers are the size of houses, and insects are as big as cars. Describe your journey through this giant garden. What amazing sights do you see? Maybe you encounter a huge bumblebee and learn about pollination, or find yourself navigating a maze of gigantic roots. How do you interact with the giant creatures and plants? Think about the adventures and challenges you face in this oversized world, like crossing a vast puddle that seems like a lake or climbing a tall stalk of grass. This prompt invites you to see the natural world from a completely different perspective, full of wonder and new discoveries.

Clarifying Questions:

1. What surprising things do you learn about garden life from this tiny perspective?

2. How do you overcome the challenges of being so small in such a big world?

3. If you could bring one small item back to your normal size as a souvenir from the garden, what would it be?

Optional Activity:
Draw a scene from your adventure in the giant's garden, showcasing the enormous plants and insects from your tiny perspective.

CHAPTER 32

THE WHISPERING WINDS

Prompt:
Every gust of wind carries whispers of the world's history. What tales do
you hear on a windy day?

To Get You Started:

I MAGINE THAT WITH EVERY breeze and gust of wind, there are whispers of the past carried through the air. On a particularly windy day, you listen closely and hear the echoes of history. What stories do the winds tell you? Maybe they carry the voices of ancient civilizations, recounting tales of great battles, lost cities, or significant events. Perhaps you hear the soft murmurs of nature's own history, like the growth of ancient forests or the formation of mountains. Describe the tales and secrets you uncover with each whispering wind. How do these stories change your understanding of the world and its history? This prompt invites you to blend imagination with historical knowledge, creating a magical connection between the past and the present.

Clarifying Questions:

1. How do you feel as you listen to the stories carried by the wind?

2. What is the most surprising or intriguing tale you hear?

3. If you could respond to one of the whispers, what would you say and why?

Optional Activity:

Create a wind chime or a simple paper windmill. As it moves with the wind, write a story or a poem inspired by the imagined whispers you hear.

CHAPTER 33

THE FRIENDLY MONSTER

Prompt:
There's a monster under your bed, but it's friendly! Write about your
adventures together.

To Get You Started:

I MAGINE DISCOVERING THAT THE monster under your bed isn't scary at all – it's actually quite friendly! Describe what the monster looks like. Is it big or small, fluffy or smooth, colorful or dark? What's its name? Think about the fun and exciting adventures you embark on with your new monster friend. Maybe you explore mysterious worlds at night, go on secret missions around the house, or even travel to other dimensions. How do you communicate with each other? What challenges do you face together, and how do you overcome them? Also, consider the special bond you form with your monster friend. This prompt invites you to turn the traditional idea of a 'monster' into a story of friendship, adventure, and understanding.

Clarifying Questions:

1. What unique abilities or special powers does your monster friend have?

2. How does having a monster friend change your daily life?

3. If your monster friend could grant you one wish, what would it be and why?

Optional Activity:

Draw a picture of your friendly monster and write a diary entry about one of your adventures together. Include details about what you did and how you felt.

CHAPTER 34

THE INVISIBLE COLOR KINGDOM

Prompt:
You discover a hidden kingdom where everything is invisible until you
add color to it. How do you bring this world to life?

To Get You Started:

I MAGINE STUMBLING UPON A mysterious kingdom where everything – from buildings to trees to animals – is completely invisible. In this kingdom, it's up to you to bring color and visibility to the world. You have a magical paintbrush that can make the invisible visible with vibrant colors.

Clarifying Questions:

1. As you color the kingdom, what inspires your choices for different colors and patterns? Do you choose them based on your favorite colors, the emotions they evoke, or perhaps the reactions of the kingdom's inhabitants?

2. How do the inhabitants of the kingdom respond to the new colors in their environment? Do they have favorite colors or preferences, and how do these colors affect their daily lives and interactions?

3. After you finish adding color to the kingdom, how do you reflect on the changes you've made? Do you feel like you've improved the kingdom, or do you have any regrets about altering its original state?

Optional Activity:

Create a 'Before and After' art project. Draw two versions of a scene from the Invisible Color Kingdom – one as it looks in its invisible state and the other after you've added colors with your magical paintbrush. This activity allows you to visualize the transformation and the power of creativity in bringing a world to life.

CHAPTER 35

THE ANCIENT PYRAMID ADVENTURE

Prompt:
You're an explorer discovering an ancient pyramid. What mysteries do you uncover?

To Get You Started:

I MAGINE YOURSELF AS A daring explorer who has just found an ancient, hidden pyramid. As you step inside, you find yourself in a world of long-lost secrets and ancient history. What does the inside of the pyramid look like? Are there hieroglyphics on the walls, hidden chambers, or maybe traps left by those who built it? Describe the artifacts and treasures you discover – could there be golden statues, mysterious relics, or even a pharaoh's tomb? Think about the challenges you face as you navigate through the labyrinth-like interior. What puzzles or riddles do you solve to unlock its secrets? Also, consider what you learn about the people who built the pyramid and their culture. This prompt invites you to weave a tale of adventure, archaeology, and discovery.

Clarifying Questions:

1. How do you prepare for your exploration into the pyramid, and what tools do you use?

2. What is the most surprising or unexpected discovery you make inside the pyramid?

3. If you could take one artifact back to study, ensuring it's preserved and respected, what would it be?

Optional Activity:

Draw a map of the pyramid as you explore it, marking the different chambers, traps, and treasures you find along the way.

CHAPTER 36

THE MAGIC CARPET RIDE

Prompt:
You have a magic carpet that can take you anywhere. Where do you go and
what do you see?

To Get You Started:

IMAGINE OWNING A MAGIC carpet that can whisk you away to any place in the blink of an eye. Where is the first place you choose to visit? You could soar above the clouds to distant lands, glide over oceans and mountains, or even explore outer space! Describe your journey on the magic carpet. What incredible sights do you see from above? Maybe you fly over the pyramids of Egypt, the bustling streets of New York City, or the serene landscapes of the Himalayas. Think about the people or creatures you might meet on your travels. Also, consider what you learn from seeing the world from this unique perspective. This prompt invites you to embark on a global adventure, exploring different cultures, landscapes, and wonders of the world.

Clarifying Questions:

1. What feelings do you experience as you travel on the magic carpet?

2. How do you choose your destinations, and what drives your curiosity?

3. If you could take someone with you on the magic carpet, who would it be and why?

Optional Activity:
Create a travel journal with entries and illustrations for each destination you visit on your magic carpet. Include descriptions of the sights, sounds, and people you encounter.

CHAPTER 37

THE SECRET GARDEN

Prompt:
You discover a secret garden with magical properties. Describe the garden
and its magic.

To Get You Started:

I MAGINE STUMBLING UPON A hidden garden that's unlike any place you've ever seen. This secret garden is filled with magical wonders. What does it look like? Are there flowers that glow and change colors, trees that whisper secrets, or perhaps a fountain that tells stories? Describe the layout of the garden – maybe there are labyrinthine paths, a clearing with a mystical pond, or vines that move and create different paths. What kind of magical properties does the garden possess? Does it have the power to heal, to change the seasons, or to transport you to different realms? Think about the creatures that might inhabit this magical place – talking animals, fairies, or mythical beings. Also, consider how you interact with the garden's magic and the adventures or discoveries you make within its confines.

Clarifying Questions:

1. How does the garden change as you explore it? Do new areas reveal themselves?

2. What emotions do you feel as you wander through the garden and experience its magic?

3. If you could take one element of the garden's magic back to the outside world, what would it be?

Optional Activity:

Draw a map or a series of pictures of the secret garden, highlighting its magical areas and inhabitants. Add descriptions or stories about each magical element you include.

CHAPTER 38

THE KINGDOM IN THE CLOUDS

Prompt:
Imagine a kingdom floating in the clouds. Who lives there and what are their customs?

To Get You Started:

H IGH ABOVE THE EARTH, nestled among the clouds, lies a mysterious kingdom. This sky-bound realm is unlike anything on the ground below. Describe what the kingdom looks like. Are the buildings crafted from clouds, do rainbows form bridges between floating islands, or are there palaces that shimmer like the sun? Think about the inhabitants of this aerial kingdom. Are they humans with the power of flight, cloud-dwelling creatures, or perhaps ethereal beings made of mist and light? Explore their customs and way of life. How do they travel from place to place, what kinds of food do they eat, and what are their traditions? Maybe they have festivals that celebrate the different types of clouds, or perhaps they can control the weather. Also, consider how they interact with the world below and what secrets or wisdom they might hold about the skies.

Clarifying Questions:

1. How do you discover the Kingdom in the Clouds, and what is your first impression when you see it?

2. What kind of challenges do the inhabitants face living in the sky, and how do they overcome them?

3. If you could bring back a souvenir or a piece of knowledge from the cloud kingdom, what would it be?

Optional Activity:
Draw a detailed picture or a series of illustrations of the Kingdom in the Clouds, showing its inhabitants, architecture, and unique aspects of their culture.

CHAPTER 39

THE POTION MAKER

Prompt:
You're a young alchemist experimenting with magical potions. Describe
your most surprising creation.

To Get You Started:

A S A BUDDING YOUNG alchemist, you've been experimenting with various magical ingredients to create potions with extraordinary effects. Describe your laboratory – is it filled with bubbling cauldrons, shelves of colorful ingredients, or ancient books of alchemical recipes? What is the most surprising potion you create? Maybe it's a potion that allows you to understand animal languages, one that changes the color of anything it touches, or perhaps a brew that can transport you to your dreams. Talk about how you come up with the idea for this potion, the process of making it, and the trial and error involved. What happens when you finally test it out? Also, consider what you learn from this experience about magic, science, and the power of curiosity.

Clarifying Questions:

1. What ingredients do you use in your most surprising potion, and where do you get them from?

2. How do you react when your potion works (or doesn't work) as expected?

3. If you could share your potion with someone, who would it be and why?

Optional Activity:

Draw a comic strip or a series of illustrations showing the process of creating your potion, from gathering ingredients to the final result of the experiment.

CHAPTER 40

THE LAND OF GIANTS

Prompt:
Imagine a world where you're the smallest person, living among giants.
What are your experiences?

To Get You Started:

P ICTURE YOURSELF IN A land where everything is on a colossal scale because it is inhabited by giants. In this world, you are tiny in comparison, navigating a world of towering beings and gigantic structures. Describe what it feels like to live in a place where everyday objects are enormous and simple tasks become adventurous challenges. How do you interact with the giants – are they friendly, oblivious to your presence, or something else? What kind of dwellings or tools do you create to adapt to your size? Share your adventures in this land – maybe you hitch a ride on a giant's pet, explore a massive garden as if it's a jungle, or find creative ways to communicate with the giants. Think about what you learn from living in a world so different from your own in terms of scale and perspective.

Clarifying Questions:

1. What is the most surprising aspect of living in a land of giants?

2. How do you overcome the challenges posed by your small size in a giant's world?

3. If you could bring one giant-sized item back to your normal-sized world, what would it be?

Optional Activity:

Draw a scene from your life in the Land of Giants, showing how you interact with the giant surroundings and inhabitants.

CHAPTER 41

THE STARRY NIGHT ADVENTURE

Prompt:
One night, the stars lead you to a hidden place. What do you discover?

To Get You Started:

O N A CLEAR AND starry night, you notice the stars twinkling in a pattern that seems to beckon you to follow. Imagine embarking on a nocturnal adventure, guided by the stars. Where do they lead you? Perhaps it's to a hidden grove that glows with bioluminescent plants, a secret beach where the sand sparkles like the night sky, or an ancient ruin that reveals a forgotten piece of history under the moonlight. Describe your journey under the starlit sky and the hidden place you discover. What secrets does it hold? Are there mystical creatures, hidden treasures, or inscriptions that tell a story of the past? Think about the sights, sounds, and feelings you experience in this magical place and the wonders you uncover.

Clarifying Questions:

1. What emotions do you feel as you follow the stars to this hidden place?

2. How do the stars guide you? Do they form a map, change colors, or move in a certain direction?

3. What lesson or knowledge do you take away from this starry night adventure?

Optional Activity:
Create a star map showing the pattern of stars that led you to the hidden place. Alongside, write a short story or a description of your adventure and discovery.

CHAPTER 42

THE OGRE'S TREASURE

Prompt:
You stumble upon a treasure map leading to a ogre's treasure. What
challenges do you face on your quest?

To Get You Started:

I MAGINE FINDING AN OLD, mysterious map that points to a treasure hidden by a ogre. This isn't just any treasure; it's said to be filled with items of unimaginable size and value. As you embark on this quest, describe the journey the map takes you on. Where does it lead? Perhaps through dense, oversized forests, across treacherous mountain paths, or into deep, unexplored caves. Think about the obstacles and challenges you face along the way. These could be natural barriers like rivers and canyons, creatures guarding the treasure, or riddles and puzzles left by the giant to protect the loot. How do you overcome these challenges? Also, consider what you find when you reach the treasure. Is it gold and jewels of enormous size, ancient artifacts, or something unexpected?

Clarifying Questions:

1. Who or what do you encounter on your journey to find the ogre's treasure?

2. How do you feel as you get closer to finding the treasure, and how do you prepare for what you might find?

3. If you could take only one item from the treasure, what would it be and why?

Optional Activity:
Draw the treasure map with landmarks and challenges marked on it. Next to it, illustrate a scene from one of the key moments of your adventure.

CHAPTER 43

THE MAGIC ZOO

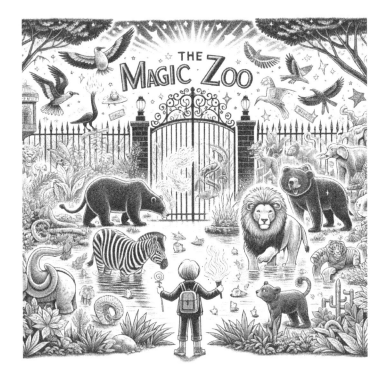

Prompt:

A zoo where the animals have magical powers. What powers do they have
and what stories do they tell?

To Get You Started:

I MAGINE VISITING A ZOO unlike any other, where each animal possesses unique magical powers. As you walk through this magical zoo, describe the different animals and the extraordinary abilities they have. Maybe there's a lion that can turn invisible, a parrot that can see into the future, or a bear that can teleport. How do these powers affect their behaviors and interactions with visitors? Think about the stories these magical animals might share. Perhaps the elephant can remember its past lives, or the monkey knows the secret language of the forest. Explore the adventures you have in this zoo – do you help solve a mystery, learn a valuable lesson, or even assist an animal in controlling its powers? Also, consider how the zookeepers care for such unique creatures.

Clarifying Questions:

1. How do you interact with the magical animals, and what do you learn from them?

2. What is the most surprising or unexpected power you encounter in one of the animals?

3. If you could take one of the magical animals on an adventure outside the zoo, which one would it be and why?

Optional Activity:
Create a magical zoo guidebook. Include illustrations and descriptions of the animals, their powers, and any special stories or legends associated with them.

CHAPTER 44

THE FOUR SEASONS IN A DAY

Prompt:
Experience all four seasons in one day. Describe how the world changes
around you.

To Get You Started:

I MAGINE A DAY WHERE the world experiences the magic of all four seasons within 24 hours. Begin with the freshness of spring in the morning. How does the world awaken? Are there flowers blooming instantly, birds chirping melodiously, and a gentle warmth in the air? As the day progresses to afternoon, summer arrives. What changes do you notice? Maybe there's a bright sun in the sky, people heading to beaches, or the sound of children playing in parks. In the evening, autumn makes its entrance. Describe the transformation of the trees into a tapestry of reds and oranges, the cool breeze, and the smell of pumpkin and spices. Finally, as night falls, winter brings its chill. How does the landscape change? Are there snowflakes gently falling, the world turning quiet and serene under a blanket of snow? This prompt invites you to explore the beauty and uniqueness of each season and how they transform the environment and mood around you.'

Clarifying Questions:

1. How do people and animals react to this rapid change of seasons?

2. What activities do you do in each season, and how do they differ?

3. Which season do you enjoy the most in this rapid cycle and why?

Optional Activity:
Draw four scenes representing each season as it appears throughout the day. Show the changes in the environment, people's activities, and wildlife.

CHAPTER 45

THE LOST KINGDOM OF ATLANTIS

Prompt:
You discover the legendary lost city of Atlantis. What do you see and who do you meet?

To Get You Started:

I MAGINE FINDING THE LONG-LOST city of Atlantis, submerged deep beneath the ocean waves. As you explore this mysterious underwater kingdom, describe what you encounter. What does Atlantis look like? Are the buildings encrusted with coral and gems, do shimmering bubbles form pathways, or are there glowing sea creatures illuminating the city? Think about who you meet in Atlantis. Are they descendants of the original Atlanteans, merpeople, or perhaps a new species entirely? What stories do they tell about their history, their culture, and how they survived hidden for so long? Explore the marvels of Atlantis – their technology, their connection with marine life, and their secrets of the deep sea. Consider how this discovery changes your understanding of history and the mysteries of the ocean.

Clarifying Questions:

1. How do the Atlanteans react to your arrival, and how do you communicate with them?

2. What is the most fascinating aspect of Atlantean technology or magic you encounter?

3. If you could bring back one piece of knowledge or item from Atlantis, what would it be?

Optional Activity:

Draw a map or a series of sketches of Atlantis, including key locations like the palace, gardens, and any significant landmarks you encounter in your exploration.

CHAPTER 46

THE GARDEN OF TALKING FLOWERS

Prompt:
You find a garden where every flower can talk. What conversations do you have?

To Get You Started:

ENVISION YOURSELF WANDERING INTO a magical garden where every flower has the ability to speak. As you stroll through this enchanting place, every type of flower has a different voice and personality. What do the flowers talk about? Maybe the roses share stories of romance and beauty, the daisies discuss the sunny days they love, or the tulips tell tales from faraway lands. Think about the questions you would ask them. How do they feel about bees and butterflies, or what insights do they offer about nature and life? Maybe some flowers offer wise advice, while others crack jokes or sing melodies. Consider what you learn from these floral conversations and how they change your view of the natural world.

Clarifying Questions:

1. Which flower do you find the most interesting or surprising, and why?

2. How do the conversations with the flowers affect your appreciation for nature?

3. If you could take one of the talking flowers home, which one would it be and what would you talk about?

Optional Activity:

Draw a picture of the Garden of Talking Flowers, illustrating the different flowers and including speech bubbles for some of their conversations.

CHAPTER 47

THE ENDLESS LIBRARY

Prompt:
You are in a library with infinite books. Describe some of the most interesting books you find.

To Get You Started:

I MAGINE WALKING INTO A grand library where the shelves stretch on endlessly, filled with books of every imaginable type. In this library, every book that was ever written, and even those that haven't been, exist. As you explore this infinite library, describe some of the most intriguing and unusual books you find. Maybe there's a book that contains every dream anyone has ever had, a tome that tells the story of a parallel universe, or a volume where the characters come to life off the pages. Consider finding ancient spellbooks, futuristic science texts, or interactive books that transport you into their stories. Think about how you navigate this endless library and the mysteries and wonders you uncover within its limitless rows of books.

Clarifying Questions:

1. How do you choose which books to explore in such an extensive library?

2. What emotions or thoughts do these extraordinary books evoke in you?

3. If you could take one book out of the endless library, which one would it be and why?

Optional Activity:

Draw a section of the endless library, including some of the unique books you describe. Add labels or a short description for each book, highlighting its special features.

CHAPTER 48

THE LABYRINTH OF MYSTERIES

Prompt:
You enter a labyrinth full of mysteries and puzzles. Describe your journey
to find the center.

To Get You Started:

I MAGINE FINDING YOURSELF AT the entrance of a vast labyrinth. As soon as you step inside, you realize this is no ordinary maze, but a labyrinth filled with riddles, puzzles, and secrets waiting to be uncovered. Describe the path you take through the twisting corridors and the challenges you encounter. Maybe there are doors that only open when a riddle is solved, walls that shift when certain levers are pulled, or optical illusions that test your perception. Think about the clues you discover along the way and how they help you navigate the labyrinth. What kind of mystical or surprising elements do you find? Perhaps there are rooms that transport you to different environments, like a dense jungle or a room full of mirrors. Also, consider the emotions and thoughts you experience as you delve deeper into the labyrinth. What do you find at the center, and what does the journey teach you?

Clarifying Questions:

1. How do you approach the challenges and puzzles in the labyrinth? Do you rely on logic, intuition, or a bit of both?

2. What is the most difficult obstacle you face, and how do you overcome it?

3. How does reaching the center of the labyrinth change your perspective or understanding of the journey?

Optional Activity:

Draw a map of the labyrinth, including some of the puzzles and challenges you faced. Add notes or symbols to represent key moments or discoveries.

CHAPTER 49

THE WIZARD SCHOOL

Prompt:
You are a student at a school for wizards. What spells do you learn and
what magical mishaps happen?

To Get You Started:

P ICTURE YOURSELF AS A student at an enchanting school for wizards. This is a place where magic is not just a fantasy, but a subject to be studied and mastered. Describe the school environment – are there floating books, talking portraits, or perhaps classrooms that change their appearance? What kinds of spells and magical skills do you learn? Maybe you start with basic spells like levitation or transformation, then progress to more complex magic like elemental control or potion brewing. Consider the teachers and classmates you interact with – are they wise and experienced, quirky and unpredictable, or stern and demanding? Share some of the magical mishaps that occur, which are common in a school of wizardry. Perhaps a spell goes wrong, turning someone into a frog, or a potion class ends in a colorful explosion. How do you and your friends handle these situations?

Clarifying Questions:

1. What is your favorite magical subject or spell, and why?

2. How do you overcome the challenges of learning magic?

3. If you could use one spell you learned in your everyday life, which one would it be?

Optional Activity:
Create a wizard school yearbook page. Include illustrations or descriptions of your favorite classes, spells, teachers, and any memorable mishaps.

CHAPTER 50

THE ENCHANTED FOREST RACE

Prompt:
You're in a race through an enchanted forest filled with obstacles and magical creatures. Describe your experience.

To Get You Started:

I MAGINE YOURSELF PARTICIPATING IN an exciting race through an enchanted forest. This isn't just any race; the forest is a labyrinth of magical wonders and challenges. Describe the setting of the forest – are there towering trees with whispering leaves, mysterious fog that shifts directions, or glowing flowers that light your path? What kinds of obstacles do you encounter? Maybe you have to cross a river with stepping stones that move, find your way through a maze of thorns, or outwit a riddle-spouting sphinx. Think about the magical creatures you meet – are they helpful, mischievous, or perhaps a bit of both? How do they affect your progress in the race? Consider your strategy for navigating the forest and the skills you use, like quick thinking, bravery, or perhaps a bit of magic of your own. What do you find at the end of the race, and what do you learn from this enchanted adventure?

Clarifying Questions:

1. What is the most unexpected obstacle or creature you encounter, and how do you overcome it?

2. Who are your companions in the race, and how do you work together?

3. If you could take one magical item from the forest to remember your race, what would it be?

Optional Activity:

Draw a map of the enchanted forest race, including key obstacles, creatures, and landmarks you encounter. Label each part with a brief description.

CHAPTER 51

THE SKY CASTLE

Prompt:
Imagine living in a castle in the sky. Describe your daily life and the view from above.

To Get You Started:

PICTURE YOURSELF LIVING IN a magnificent castle floating high above the clouds. This sky castle is a realm of wonder and beauty, far removed from the ordinary world below. Describe the architecture of your sky castle – does it have soaring towers, glass walkways, cloud gardens, or rooms that change with your mood? What is your daily routine like in this castle in the clouds? Maybe you have breakfast watching the sunrise above an endless sea of clouds, spend your day exploring the castle's magical rooms, or have adventures on a flying creature that takes you even higher into the sky. Describe the incredible view from your castle – the way the world looks during the day and night, the feeling of being above everything, and the sights you see, like distant lands, soaring birds, or perhaps other floating islands. Consider how living in the sky changes your perspective on life and the world below.

Clarifying Questions:

1. How do you travel to and from your sky castle, and what adventures do you have during these journeys?

2. What kind of creatures or beings live with you in the sky castle, and how do you interact with them?

3. If you could invite someone from the ground to visit your castle, who would it be and what would you show them first?

Optional Activity:

Draw a picture of your sky castle and the view from one of its towers or balconies. Include details like the landscape below, the sky around, and any magical aspects of the castle.

CHAPTER 52

THE MAGIC LANTERN

Prompt:
You find a lantern with a genie who grants you three wishes. What do you
wish for?

To Get You Started:

I MAGINE STUMBLING UPON AN old, mysterious lantern. When you rub it, a genie appears in a swirl of magical smoke, ready to grant you three wishes. Think carefully about what you wish for. Your first wish might be something personal or fun – maybe you want the ability to fly, become the best at a favorite sport, or have a secret hideout. For your second wish, you might think of others – perhaps wishing for happiness for your family, a cure for a disease, or an end to a global problem. When it comes to your third wish, consider what the genie suggests about the nature of wishes and the consequences they can have. Maybe this wish is for something unexpected, like the wisdom to make good choices, or even setting the genie free. Describe how each wish changes your life and the world around you. What adventures do you have, and what lessons do you learn about the power of wishing?

Clarifying Questions:

1. How do you feel when you meet the genie, and how do your feelings change after making each wish?

2. What considerations or dilemmas do you face before making each wish?

3. If you had the chance to make more wishes in the future, would you do anything differently?

Optional Activity:

Create a wish journal. Write down your three wishes and illustrate what happens when each wish is granted, showing how it affects you and others.

CHAPTER 53

THE LOST CITY OF GOLD

Prompt:
You embark on an adventure to find a mythical lost city of gold. Describe
your quest.

To Get You Started:

I MAGINE SETTING OFF ON a thrilling adventure to find a legendary city of gold, rumored to be hidden in a remote and uncharted part of the world. Start by describing how you hear about this mythical city and what motivates you to find it. Is it a tale passed down through generations, a cryptic map you discover, or a story you overhear from a mysterious traveler? As you begin your journey, think about the diverse landscapes you traverse – dense jungles with towering trees, treacherous mountains, or vast deserts with endless sands. What challenges do you face along the way? Perhaps you encounter natural obstacles like rivers and canyons, puzzles and traps left by ancient protectors of the city, or rival adventurers also seeking the gold. Describe your feelings as you get closer to your goal and the excitement of uncovering clues. What do you find when you finally reach the city? Is it a place of unimaginable wealth, a forgotten civilization with hidden knowledge, or something completely unexpected?

Clarifying Questions:

1. What kind of preparations do you make for your journey, and who, if anyone, accompanies you?

2. How do you overcome the most significant challenge on your quest?

3. What is the most valuable thing (tangible or intangible) you find in the lost city of gold?

Optional Activity:

Draw a comic strip or a series of illustrations depicting key moments of your adventure, including challenges, discoveries, and the moment you find the city of gold.

CHAPTER 54

THE FESTIVAL OF COLORS

Prompt:
You're at a festival where everything is bright and colorful. Describe the
sights, sounds, and activities.

To Get You Started:

I MAGINE BEING AT A lively and joyous festival where colors play a central role in the celebration. The entire place is a canvas of vibrant hues, with bright decorations adorning every corner. Describe the array of colors you see – are there streamers and balloons in every shade, buildings painted with vivid murals, or people wearing colorful costumes and masks? Talk about the sounds that fill the air. Is there lively music that makes everyone want to dance, the laughter and chatter of people enjoying themselves, or perhaps the sound of drums and other instruments? Consider the activities and events at the festival. Maybe there's a parade with elaborately decorated floats, contests for the best-dressed in colorful attire, or stalls where you can paint and create your own colorful crafts. Don't forget to describe the delicious foods – are there brightly colored treats and drinks that are as much a feast for the eyes as they are for the taste buds?

Clarifying Questions:

1. What is the most striking or beautiful sight you see at the festival?

2. How do the different colors affect your mood and the atmosphere of the festival?

3. If you could bring one element of the festival back to your daily life, what would it be?

Optional Activity:

Create a collage or a painting that captures the essence of the Festival of Colors. Use bright colors and different materials to reflect the festival's joyful and vibrant atmosphere.

CHAPTER 55

THE CASTLE OF MIRRORS

Prompt:
You explore a castle filled with mirrors that lead to different worlds.
Where do you go?

To Get You Started:

P ICTURE YOURSELF IN AN ancient, mysterious castle filled with countless mirrors of all shapes and sizes. Each mirror is a gateway to a different world or realm. Describe the moment you step through your first mirror – where does it take you? Perhaps you find yourself in a world where everything is upside-down, a realm of endless night skies filled with stars, or a land where mythical creatures roam freely. Explore the various worlds you encounter through different mirrors. How do they differ from your world, and what unique experiences do they offer? Maybe one mirror leads to a past era, while another shows a possible future. Consider how you navigate from one mirror to the next and the decisions you make about which mirror to step through. What challenges do you face in these alternate worlds, and what allies or adversaries do you meet? Also, think about the lessons you learn from each world and how they change your perspective.

Questions to Help You Make it Even Better:

1. How do you feel as you pass through each mirror, and what surprises you about the worlds you visit?

2. What is the most memorable encounter or event you experience in these mirror worlds?

3. If you could take something back from one of the mirror worlds, what would it be?

Optional Activity:

Draw a series of postcards from each world you visit through the mirrors. On each postcard, illustrate a key scene from that world and write a brief description or message on the back.

CHAPTER 56

THE MAGICAL CHRISTMAS EVE

Prompt:
Write about a magical adventure that happens on Christmas Eve. Who do you meet and what surprises do you find?

To Get You Started:

I MAGINE A CHRISTMAS EVE like no other, where a sprinkle of holiday magic leads to an unforgettable adventure. As the world settles down on this special night, something extraordinary happens to you. Describe the beginning of your magical journey – does it start with a mysterious gift, a strange visitor, or perhaps a magical snowfall that seems to beckon you outside? Who do you meet on your adventure? Maybe you encounter talking animals preparing for Christmas in their own way, elves on a secret mission, or even Santa Claus himself in need of assistance. Explore the surprises and wonders you discover – a hidden winter wonderland, a flying sleigh ride around the world, or a peek into Santa's workshop. Consider the sights, sounds, and smells of this magical night and how they amplify the spirit of Christmas. What lessons do you learn about the true meaning of the holiday, and what special memories do you create?

Clarifying Questions:

1. What is the most magical moment of your Christmas Eve adventure, and how does it make you feel?

2. How do the characters you meet contribute to your understanding of the holiday spirit?

3. If you could keep one magical souvenir from your adventure, what would it be?

Optional Activity:

Create a holiday card or a drawing depicting a scene from your magical Christmas Eve adventure. Include details about the characters and the magical elements you encountered.

CHAPTER 57

THE ICE CREAM MOUNTAIN

Prompt:
You discover a mountain made entirely of ice cream. Describe your delicious adventure.

To Get You Started:

IMAGINE STUMBLING UPON A colossal mountain made entirely of ice cream. This isn't just a small hill of ice cream, but a towering mountain with scoops of every flavor imaginable. Describe your first reaction to seeing this delicious wonder. What flavors make up the mountain? Maybe there are layers of classic vanilla, chocolate, and strawberry, or more exotic flavors like mango, pistachio, or bubble gum. Consider the journey you undertake to explore this mountain. Do you start at the bottom and work your way up, sampling different flavors as you go? Maybe you find hidden caves of frozen treats, rivers of melted sundae toppings, or even a waterfall of chocolate syrup. Think about the tools or equipment you use to navigate and sample this ice cream mountain. Also, who do you meet on your adventure? Perhaps there are other explorers, friendly animals with a sweet tooth, or even a custodian of the mountain with stories to tell about its origins. What challenges do you face in this frosty, sweet landscape?

Clarifying Questions:

1. How does each flavor of the ice cream mountain taste, and which one is your favorite?

2. What creative ways do you find to enjoy the ice cream without getting too cold or too full?

3. If you could bring back a sample of the ice cream for your friends or family, which flavor would you choose?

Optional Activity:
Draw a colorful illustration of the Ice Cream Mountain, labeling different areas with the flavors and features you encounter on your adventure.

CHAPTER 58

THE MAGIC MUSIC BOX

Prompt:

You find a music box that transports you to the world of its song. Where
do you go and what do you experience?

To Get You Started:

ENVISION DISCOVERING AN OLD, beautifully crafted music box. When you wind it up and it begins to play, you find yourself transported into the world created by its melody. Describe the music box – what does it look like, and what song does it play? As the music envelops you, imagine the world it conjures. If the song is a soft, slow melody, perhaps you find yourself in a tranquil meadow under a starlit sky. If it's a lively, upbeat tune, maybe you're taken to a bustling city with bright lights and joyous celebrations. Explore the sights, sounds, and sensations of this musical world. What adventures do you have there? Do you meet characters who are part of the song's story, or do you become the protagonist in a narrative shaped by the melody? Consider how the music influences the environment and events around you. How does the experience change when the music box plays a different song?

Clarifying Questions:

1. What emotions do you feel as you're transported by the music box's song?

2. How does the world of the song change your perspective or mood?

3. If you could choose a song for the music box to play, what would it be and why?

Optional Activity:

Draw a scene from one of the worlds you visit with the music box. Include elements that reflect the music's rhythm, mood, and story.

CHAPTER 59

THE CITY OF ROBOTS

Prompt:
Imagine a city where all residents are robots. How is it different from your city?

To Get You Started:

P ICTURE YOURSELF VISITING A city entirely inhabited by robots. This isn't a scene from a science fiction movie; it's a real place where robots of all shapes, sizes, and functions live and work. Describe what you see as you walk through the city. Are the buildings sleek and metallic, do digital displays line the streets, or are there charging stations instead of parks? Think about how the robot residents interact with each other. Is there a system of organization and efficiency that's vastly different from human cities? Consider the daily activities in the robot city – perhaps there are factories where robots build other robots, repair centers that function as hospitals, or data hubs where robots exchange information. How do these robots spend their leisure time, if they have any? Compare this city to your own. What are the most striking differences and similarities? What can humans learn from the way robots live and organize their city?

Clarifying Questions:

1. How do you feel as you explore this city of robots, and what surprises or fascinates you the most?

2. What aspects of the robot city do you find more efficient or effective compared to human cities?

3. If you could bring back one piece of robot technology to your city, what would it be?

Optional Activity:
Draw a map or a series of illustrations showing different parts of the robot city, highlighting unique buildings, robots, and activities you encounter.

CHAPTER 60

INVENT A NEW HOLIDAY

Prompt:
What is the holiday, and how is it celebrated?

To Get You Started:

I MAGINE YOU HAVE THE chance to create a brand new holiday. Think about what the holiday celebrates – it could be something meaningful, whimsical, or even a bit quirky. What's the name of this holiday? Describe the traditions, activities, and customs associated with it. For example, if it's a holiday celebrating friendship, there might be activities like a friend exchange, where you do something nice for a friend's friend, or a community event where stories about friendship are shared. If it's a holiday that celebrates the wonders of the natural world, there could be outdoor expeditions or a day of planting trees. Think about the foods that are eaten on this holiday, any special decorations used, and how people greet each other. Is there a particular dress code or color scheme? Also, consider how this holiday impacts the community and brings people together. What message or values do you hope this new holiday promotes?

Clarifying Questions:

1. How do families and friends gather and celebrate your holiday?

2. What unique or unusual traditions are part of the holiday?

3. If your holiday had a symbol or emblem, what would it be?

Optional Activity:

Create a poster or an invitation for your new holiday. Include the name of the holiday, a brief description of how it's celebrated, and any important symbols or colors associated with it.

CHAPTER 61

THE ULTIMATE TREEHOUSE

Prompt:
Design your dream treehouse and describe the adventures you have in it.

To Get You Started:

I MAGINE YOU HAVE THE opportunity to create the ultimate treehouse, a place straight out of your wildest dreams. Start by describing the treehouse's design. How many levels does it have? What materials is it made of – sturdy oak, magical wood, or something else? What special features does it include – rope bridges, secret rooms, slides, or perhaps telescopes for stargazing? Think about the rooms and what each one is used for. Maybe there's a room filled with games and toys, a cozy reading nook, or even a laboratory for experiments. Consider the adventures that take place in and around your treehouse. Do you have treasure hunts, defend against pretend invaders, or use it as a base for exploring the surrounding area? What kind of creatures or characters do you encounter? Also, think about how your treehouse serves as a magical escape, a place of fun, learning, and imagination.

Clarifying Questions:

1. How do you access your treehouse – is it by climbing, a ladder, or perhaps a magical elevator?

2. What is your favorite activity or feature in the treehouse?

3. If you could share your treehouse with anyone in the world, who would it be and why?

Optional Activity:

Draw a blueprint or a detailed illustration of your ultimate treehouse, labeling each room and feature. Next to it, write a short story or diary entry about a day spent in your treehouse.

CHAPTER 62

THE BOOK OF SECRETS

Prompt:
You find a mysterious book that has answers to every question. What do
you ask it?

To Get You Started:

I MAGINE DISCOVERING A REMARKABLE book, ancient and bound in mystery, known as the Book of Secrets. This book possesses the incredible ability to answer any question asked of it. Describe your first encounter with the book – where do you find it, and what does it look like? Is it in an old library, hidden in an attic, or discovered in an antique store? Think about the questions you decide to ask. Do you seek knowledge about the universe, the secrets of history, solutions to unsolved mysteries, or insight into the future? Maybe you ask personal questions about your life path or seek advice on a challenge you're facing. Consider how the book's answers impact you. Are they straightforward, or do they come in riddles or parables? What emotions do you experience as you uncover these truths? Also, think about the responsibility that comes with such knowledge. How do you use or share the information you gain from the Book of Secrets?

Clarifying Questions:

1. How do you decide which questions are most important to ask?

2. What is the most surprising or unexpected answer you receive?

3. If you could share one piece of knowledge from the book with the world, what would it be?

Optional Activity:

Create a diary entry or a series of notes detailing the most significant questions you ask the book and the answers you receive. Illustrate your reactions or the changes these answers bring to your life.

CHAPTER 63

THE FRIENDLY GHOST

Prompt:
A friendly ghost lives in your attic. Write about your adventures and
conversations together.

To Get You Started:

I MAGINE DISCOVERING THAT A friendly ghost resides in your attic. This isn't a scary ghost, but a kind and curious one, perhaps from a different time period. Describe your first encounter with the ghost – how do you react, and how does the ghost introduce itself? Think about the adventures you have together. Maybe the ghost shows you glimpses of the past, shares hidden secrets of your house, or takes you on ethereal adventures where you float through walls and explore unseen places. What conversations do you have with the ghost? It might tell you stories of its life, share wisdom, or even help you with problems you're facing. Consider how your friendship with the ghost changes your perspective on life and the afterlife. What fun, spooky, or enlightening experiences do you share, and how do you help each other?

Clarifying Questions:

1. What is the most surprising thing you learn from the ghost?

2. How do you keep your friendship with the ghost a secret, or do you tell others about it?

3. If the ghost could grant you one wish, what would it be?

Optional Activity:

Draw a comic strip or a series of illustrations about a memorable adventure or conversation with your friendly attic ghost. Include speech bubbles and captions to capture the dialogue and story.

CHAPTER 64

THE INVISIBLE ISLAND

Prompt:
An invisible island appears once every decade. What do you find when you explore it?

To Get You Started:

I MAGINE AN ISLAND THAT is invisible to the world, appearing only once every ten years. As one of the few to witness its emergence, describe your journey to this elusive island. How do you find it – is it through ancient maps, mystical guidance, or sheer luck? Once you arrive, depict the island's landscape and environment. What unique features does it have? Maybe there are exotic plants that glow, animals thought to be extinct, or ancient ruins holding secrets of a lost civilization. Explore the mysteries and wonders you uncover on the island. Are there hidden treasures, magical artifacts, or inscriptions telling of the island's history? Think about the challenges you face while exploring – perhaps navigating through a dense, enchanted forest or deciphering riddles to unlock hidden areas. Consider the emotions you experience as you uncover the island's secrets and the impact of your discoveries on your understanding of the world.

Clarifying Questions:

1. How does the island change or reveal itself during your exploration?

2. What is the most extraordinary thing you find on the island?

3. If you could take one item from the island back with you, what would it be?

Optional Activity:

Draw a map or a series of sketches of the invisible island, highlighting key locations, discoveries, and any creatures or characters you encounter.

CHAPTER 65

THE MIRROR WORLD

Prompt:

You step into a mirror and find a world opposite to ours. What is different there?

To Get You Started::

Imagine discovering a mirror that is a portal to an alternate world – a place where everything is the opposite of your reality. As you step through the mirror, describe the initial sensations and what you see. How is this mirror world different? Perhaps time moves backward, the laws of gravity are reversed, or people speak in reverse. Explore the environment and how daily life functions in this opposite world. Maybe streets are above in the sky, buildings are upside down, or trees grow downwards from the clouds. Consider the people you meet and how their behaviors and customs differ from what you know. What adventures do you have in this topsy-turvy world? Think about the challenges you face in navigating a world where everything you're accustomed to is inverted or altered. How do you adapt, and what unique experiences do you have? Also, ponder what insights this mirror world gives you about your own world and how seeing things from an opposite perspective changes your understanding.

Clarifying Questions:

1. What is the most surprising or challenging aspect of the mirror world?

2. How do your interactions with the inhabitants of the mirror world shape your experience?

3. If you could bring one element or idea from the mirror world back to your own, what would it be?

Optional Activity:

Create a two-part illustration: one showing a scene from your world and the other depicting how it appears in the mirror world. Highlight the differences and similarities between the two.

CHAPTER 66

THE ART THAT COMES TO LIFE

Prompt:
Any drawing you make comes to life. What do you draw and what
adventures ensue?

To Get You Started:

IMAGINE POSSESSING THE EXTRAORDINARY ability to bring your drawings to life. Every time you put pencil to paper, whatever you create becomes real and steps out of the page. Think about the first thing you decide to draw – is it a friendly animal, a mythical creature, or perhaps a character from your imagination? Describe the moment your creation comes to life and your reaction to it. What adventures do you embark on with your living drawings? Maybe you draw a majestic bird and soar through the skies, sketch an underwater creature to explore ocean depths, or create a whimsical companion for a journey through an enchanted forest. Consider the interactions you have with your creations. What do they teach you about creativity, imagination, and the power of art? Also, think about the challenges that arise from bringing drawings to life and how you handle them.

Clarifying Questions:

1. How do you decide what to draw, and what inspires your creations?

2. What is the most surprising interaction you have with one of your living drawings?

3. If you could permanently bring one of your drawings to life, which one would it be and why?

Optional Activity:

Create a series of drawings that represent your living creations. Next to each drawing, write a short description or story about the adventure or experience you have with it.

CHAPTER 67

THE CHOCOLATE RIVER

Prompt:
You find a river made of chocolate. Describe your journey along this sweet river.

To Get You Started:

I MAGINE STUMBLING UPON A wondrous river flowing with rich, creamy chocolate instead of water. Describe your initial reaction upon discovering this chocolate river. Is it a dark, milk, or perhaps a white chocolate river? How does it smell, and what is the texture like? Consider how you decide to explore along this unique river. Maybe you fashion a boat out of a giant leaf or a hollowed-out piece of candy and set off downstream. Describe the sights you see along the riverbanks – are there trees with candy leaves, bushes with marshmallow blooms, or perhaps wildlife enjoying the chocolate as well? Think about the adventures you have on this river. Do you stop to sample delicious treats along the way, find a waterfall of cascading chocolate, or meet other explorers or creatures drawn to the river? Also, consider the source of the chocolate river. Does it come from a magical spring, a hidden factory, or is it part of a chocolatey natural wonder?

Clarifying Questions:

1. What challenges or surprises do you encounter on your chocolate river journey?

2. How do you feel as you travel along the river, and what delights you the most?

3. If you could bring back a souvenir from your chocolate river adventure, what would it be?

Optional Activity:

Draw a map or a series of scenes depicting your journey along the chocolate river, highlighting key experiences and discoveries.

CHAPTER 68

THE UNDERGROUND KINGDOM

Prompt:
You discover a kingdom beneath the Earth. What is life like there?

To Get You Started:

I MAGINE UNCOVERING A SECRET passage that leads to an astonishing underground kingdom. As you descend, describe the transition from the surface world to this subterranean realm. What does this hidden kingdom look like? Are there luminous crystals lighting the caverns, buildings carved into the walls of vast underground chambers, or rivers and lakes that glow with an ethereal light? Explore the culture and daily life of the kingdom's inhabitants. What are their homes like, what do they eat, and how do they spend their time? Maybe they have developed unique technologies or magic suited to their underground environment. Consider the societal structure – is there a ruler or a council, and how do they interact with the surface world, if at all? Think about the adventures you have in this kingdom. Do you discover ancient secrets, encounter rare creatures, or help solve a problem threatening the kingdom?

Clarifying Questions:

1. How do the underground kingdom's inhabitants adapt to living beneath the Earth?

2. What is the most surprising or unique aspect of this kingdom compared to the surface world?

3. If you could bring one item or piece of knowledge back to the surface, what would it be?

Optional Activity:
Draw a detailed illustration or a series of sketches of the underground kingdom, showing key locations, inhabitants, and any unique features or activities.

CHAPTER 69

THE WISE OWL'S RIDDLES

Prompt:
A wise owl gives you three riddles to solve. What are they and how do you
solve them?

To Get You Started:

I MAGINE ENCOUNTERING A WISE old owl in a serene forest. This owl, known for its wisdom, poses three challenging riddles to you. Each riddle is a test of wit and insight. As you ponder each riddle, consider how you feel – are you puzzled, intrigued, or excited?

The first riddle might be about something in nature, the second about something man-made, and the third a test of your understanding of the world or human nature. Think about how you approach solving these riddles. Do you use logic, look for hidden meanings, or draw on your knowledge and experiences?

Reflect on how each solution comes to you. Is it an 'aha' moment, or do you struggle and need to ask the owl for hints? Consider what the owl's riddles and their answers teach you about observation, perspective, and the mysteries of the world.

After solving the riddles, imagine how the wise owl reacts. Does it offer you words of wisdom, a secret about the forest, or perhaps a clue to a hidden treasure or a new adventure? How does this encounter with the wise owl and the riddles change your perspective or understanding of the world around you?

Clarifying Questions:

1. What strategies or thought processes help you solve the riddles?

2. How do the riddles and their answers affect your view of wisdom and knowledge?

3. If you could ask the wise owl a question in return, what would it be?

Optional Activity:

Create a riddle journal. Write down the riddles posed by the wise owl and your answers to them. Next to each riddle, illustrate your thought process or the moment of revelation when you figured out the answer.

CHAPTER 70

THE LIVING PAINTINGS

Prompt:
Paintings in a museum come to life and tell their stories. What stories do
they tell?

To Get You Started:

I MAGINE VISITING A MUSEUM where, in a magical moment, the paintings on the walls come to life. Each painting has a story to tell, a moment frozen in time now given a voice. Describe the paintings you encounter and the stories they share. Perhaps a landscape painting depicts a historic battle, and it tells you the tale of heroism and strategy. Maybe a portrait comes to life to recount the life story of the person it depicts, sharing secrets of their past, or a still life painting explains the significance of each item captured on the canvas. Consider the variety of eras, styles, and subjects of the paintings. How do these stories enrich your understanding of history, art, and the human experience? Think about how the museum visitors react to this extraordinary phenomenon. What emotions and thoughts does this experience evoke in you?

Clarifying Questions:

1. Which painting's story resonates with you the most, and why?

2. How do the stories of the paintings change your perception of the artwork?

3. If you could step into one of the paintings to experience its story firsthand, which one would it be?

Optional Activity:

Draw or paint a scene inspired by one of the stories told by the living paintings. Write a short narrative or description alongside it to capture the essence of the story.

CHAPTER 71

JOURNEY TO THE CENTER OF THE EARTH

Prompt:
Describe your adventure as you travel to the center of the Earth. What wonders or dangers do you encounter?

To Get You Started:

I MAGINE EMBARKING ON AN extraordinary journey to the center of the Earth. The adventure begins with finding a hidden passage or a deep cave that leads deep into the earth's crust. Describe your preparations for this journey and the equipment you bring – perhaps special gear for climbing, tools for navigating through dark tunnels, or instruments for scientific measurements. As you travel deeper, depict the changing landscapes and environments you encounter. Maybe you pass through layers of ancient rock formations, discover underground rivers or lakes, or come across caverns filled with glowing crystals. Consider the wonders as well as the dangers you face – beautiful but unfamiliar ecosystems, rare creatures, extreme temperatures, or precarious paths. Think about any companions who join you on your journey and how you work together to overcome challenges. What mysteries or secrets about our planet do you uncover, and how do these discoveries change your view of the Earth?

Clarifying Questions:

1. What is the most impressive thing you see on your journey?

2. How do you navigate and communicate in the depths of the Earth?

3. What is the most important lesson or insight you gain from this journey?

Optional Activity:

Create a journal entry or a series of diary pages documenting key moments of your journey to the center of the Earth. Include sketches of the landscapes, creatures, or phenomena you encounter.

CHAPTER 72

THE WORLD OF INVISIBILITY

Prompt:
You wake up one day and find out you are invisible. What mischief or
adventures do you get up to?

To Get You Started:

I MAGINE THE SURPRISE AND curiosity you experience when you wake up to discover that you have become invisible. At first, you might test your newfound ability, marveling at how you can move unseen by others. Consider the initial reactions of those around you when they realize they can't see you. What kind of mischief or pranks might you play? Perhaps you decide to spook your friends with objects that seem to move on their own, or you play the role of a secret helper, assisting people without their knowledge. Think about the adventures you could embark on while invisible. You might explore places you normally couldn't go, overhear secret conversations, or become an unseen witness to events. Also, ponder the challenges of being invisible. How do you navigate a world where no one can see you, and what do you do when you want to be noticed again? Consider how this experience changes your perspective on privacy, interaction, and the importance of being seen and acknowledged.

Clarifying Questions:

1. What is the most amusing or rewarding thing you do while invisible?

2. How do you feel about being invisible – is it exciting, lonely, or a mix of both?

3. If you had the choice, would you want to become visible again? Why or why not?

Optional Activity:
Draw a comic strip or a series of scenes showing some of the mischievous pranks or adventures you have while invisible. Add speech bubbles or captions to describe your actions and the reactions of others.

CHAPTER 73

THE ULTIMATE BIRTHDAY PARTY

Prompt:
Plan your dream birthday party. Who attends and what activities and surprises are there?

To Get You Started:

I MAGINE YOU HAVE THE opportunity to plan your ultimate dream birthday party, where anything is possible. Begin by describing the setting of your party – is it in a grand castle, a space station, an amusement park, or perhaps a beach with magical sand? Think about who you would invite. Would it be friends, family, characters from your favorite books or movies, or even famous personalities from history? Describe the activities and entertainment at your party. Maybe there are thrilling rides, mysterious magic shows, interactive virtual reality games, or a live performance by your favorite band. Consider the special surprises that make your party unique – a spectacular fireworks show, a surprise guest, or a fantastic gift that you've always wanted. Don't forget the food – what delicious treats and birthday cake await you and your guests? Describe the decorations, the music, and the overall atmosphere. How does this birthday party reflect your personality and interests, and what memorable moments do you experience?

Clarifying Questions:

1. What is the theme of your ultimate birthday party, and how is it incorporated into the decorations and activities?

2. How do the activities at your party cater to you and your guests' interests?

3. What is the highlight or most unforgettable moment of your dream birthday party?

Optional Activity:

Create an invitation for your dream birthday party. Include details like the location, guests, activities, and any special theme. Draw decorations or scenes from the party on the invitation.

CHAPTER 74

THE LITTLE MERMAID'S ADVENTURE

Prompt:
Write a story from the perspective of a little mermaid exploring the ocean.

To Get You Started:

I MAGINE YOURSELF AS A little mermaid, eager to explore the vast and mysterious world of the ocean. Begin your story by describing your home under the sea. What does it look like? Maybe it's a colorful coral reef bustling with marine life, a hidden underwater cave, or a majestic palace in an ancient, sunken city. As a mermaid, consider your unique abilities – perhaps communicating with sea creatures, swimming swiftly with a powerful tail, or creating enchanting music. Describe the wonders you see on your ocean adventures. You might encounter exotic fish, discover hidden treasures, or even come across mysterious sea monsters. Think about the challenges you face in the ocean depths, like strong currents, human pollution, or navigating the vast and sometimes perilous waters. What new friends or allies do you meet, and what dangers do you overcome? Also, consider what you learn about the ocean and its importance to the world above the waves.

Clarifying Questions:

1. What is the most exciting discovery you make during your ocean exploration?

2. How do your interactions with other sea creatures and the marine environment shape your adventure?

3. What message or treasure do you bring back to your mermaid community from your journey?

Optional Activity:
Draw a scene from your mermaid adventure, such as a beautiful coral reef, a thrilling encounter with a sea creature, or a discovery of an underwater wonder. Add a caption or a short description to explain the scene.

CHAPTER 75

THE CANDY CANE FOREST

Prompt:
Explore a forest where the trees are candy canes. What other sweet surprises do you find?

To Get You Started:

I MAGINE ENTERING A MAGICAL forest where all the trees are towering candy canes of various colors and flavors. Describe the vibrant and sweet-smelling landscape of this unique forest. Are the candy cane trees peppermint, spearmint, or fruit-flavored? Maybe they sparkle with sugary frost or have branches dripping with chocolate. As you wander through this candy forest, think about the other sweet surprises and wonders you discover. Perhaps there's a clearing with a marshmallow pond, bushes with gummy berries, or flowers made of delicate spun sugar. Consider encountering friendly creatures or characters in this forest – maybe gingerbread animals, a chocolate bunny guide, or even a sugarplum fairy. Describe the adventures you have in this forest. Do you go on a treasure hunt for the rarest candy, help a lost gingerbread person find their way, or partake in a grand feast with the forest's inhabitants? Also, ponder the challenges of a forest made of candy – does it attract ants or bees, or maybe it's at risk of melting in the sun?

Clarifying Questions:

1. What is your favorite part of the candy cane forest, and why?

2. How do the flavors and sights of the forest change your experience and adventure?

3. If you could bring back one sweet souvenir from the forest, what would it be?

Optional Activity:

Draw a map or a series of illustrations of the Candy Cane Forest, highlighting the different areas, creatures, and sweet surprises you encounter.

CHAPTER 76

THE SHRINKING POTION

Prompt:
You accidentally drink a shrinking potion and become tiny. Describe your adventures in a giant world.

To Get You Started:

I MAGINE THE SHOCK AND surprise you experience when you drink a mysterious potion and suddenly start shrinking! As you become tiny, describe how the world around you transforms. Ordinary objects now appear enormous – a pencil is like a log, a coin is a large disk, and a small puddle becomes a vast lake. Explore your new perspective in this giant world. What everyday challenges become adventures? Maybe crossing a room feels like journeying across a vast terrain, climbing onto furniture becomes a daring mountaineering expedition, or avoiding a curious pet turns into a thrilling escape. Think about how you navigate this new, larger-than-life world. Do you ride on a paper airplane, create a raft from a leaf, or communicate with insects? Consider the creative solutions you come up with to handle daily tasks. Also, imagine how you search for a way to return to your normal size. Do you seek help from friends, try to recreate the potion, or consult books that now seem like vast libraries?

Clarifying Questions:

1. What is the most exciting or challenging adventure you have while tiny?

2. How do you feel about the world and everyday objects from your new, tiny perspective?

3. If you had the chance to return to your normal size, what tiny experience would you miss the most?

Optional Activity:

Create a miniature diary entry or a series of drawings depicting your adventures as a tiny person in a giant world. Include sketches of the ingenious solutions and tools you devise to navigate this new perspective.

CHAPTER 77

THE SUPERPOWER CHOICE

Prompt:
You can choose one superpower for a day. What do you choose and how do you use it?

To Get You Started:

I MAGINE YOU HAVE THE opportunity to choose any superpower, but only for one day. What power would you pick? Would it be the ability to fly, become invisible, read minds, teleport, or something else entirely? Describe how you discover you have this one-day superpower and your initial reaction to it. Think about how you decide to use your power throughout the day. Do you use it for fun and adventure, like flying around the city, teleporting to different countries, or sneaking around invisibly? Maybe you choose to help people, using your superpower for good deeds, like rescuing those in danger, solving mysteries, or performing acts of kindness unseen. Consider the challenges or dilemmas you face while using your power. How do you keep it a secret, or do you reveal it to others? What lessons do you learn from this experience about responsibility, power, and the choices you make?

Clarifying Questions:

1. What is the first thing you do after discovering your superpower?

2. How does having a superpower for a day change your perspective on your everyday life?

3. If you had the opportunity to choose a superpower for someone else, what would it be and why?

Optional Activity:
Draw a comic strip or a storyboard showcasing a day in your life with your chosen superpower. Include scenes that highlight both the fun and challenging aspects of having a superpower.

CHAPTER 78

THE GIANT'S BACKPACK

Prompt:
You find a giant's backpack with many strange items. What do you find
and what stories do they tell?

To Get You Started:

I MAGINE COMING ACROSS A massive backpack, so large that it's almost the size of a small house, belonging to a giant. Curiosity gets the better of you, and you decide to explore its contents. As you rummage through the giant backpack, describe the unusual items you find – each item has its own story and significance. Maybe there's a map of places the giant has visited, marked with mysterious symbols and notes. Perhaps you find a gigantic feather from a mythical bird, a key to an unknown lock, or a diary filled with entries of the giant's adventures. Think about how each item gives you insight into the giant's life. What do these belongings tell you about the giant's personality, travels, interests, or friendships? Consider the emotions and thoughts that each discovery evokes in you. How do these items expand your understanding of the world and spark your own sense of adventure?

Clarifying Questions:

1. What is the most intriguing item you find in the giant's backpack, and why?

2. How do these discoveries change your perception of giants and other mythical beings?

3. If you could meet the giant to whom the backpack belongs, what would you ask or say?

Optional Activity:

Draw a collection of items found in the giant's backpack. Next to each item, write a brief description or story about its origin or significance.

CHAPTER 79

THE WORLD TURNED UPSIDE DOWN

Prompt:

One day, you wake up and everything is upside down. How do you adapt
to this new world?

To Get You Started:

I MAGINE WAKING UP TO find that the whole world has flipped upside down. The ceiling is now the floor, and everything that was once below is now above. Describe your initial reaction to this topsy-turvy change. How do you navigate this upside-down world? Consider the everyday challenges – walking on the ceiling, eating with utensils hanging from above, or reading books where the words are all reversed. Think about how you adapt to basic activities like getting dressed, watching TV, or even sleeping. How does this change affect your daily routine, and what creative solutions do you come up with? Also, consider the interactions with other people. How do they cope with this new reality, and how do you help each other? Maybe you invent new games, develop unique ways of communication, or find joy in the peculiarities of this upside-down world. Reflect on what this experience teaches you about adaptability, perspective, and finding balance in unusual circumstances.

Clarifying Questions:

1. What is the most difficult aspect of the upside-down world to adapt to?

2. How do your relationships with friends and family change in this new setting?

3. If the world were to flip back to normal, what aspect of the upside-down world would you miss or appreciate more?

Optional Activity:
Draw a series of scenes depicting life in the upside-down world. Show how ordinary activities and places look and function differently in this new reality.

CHAPTER 80

SUPERHERO STORY

Prompt:
Create your own superhero. What are their powers and how do they save
the day?

To Get You Started:

I MAGINE CREATING YOUR VERY own superhero. Start by thinking about what makes your superhero unique. What is their name, and what do they look like? Do they have a costume, and if so, what colors and symbols represent them? Now, consider their superpowers. Do they have the ability to fly, super strength, invisibility, telekinesis, or perhaps something completely original like controlling weather or transforming objects with their touch? Describe how they discovered their powers and the moment they decided to become a superhero.

Next, think about the kind of challenges and villains your superhero faces. Are they protecting their city from giant robots, stopping bank robbers, rescuing people from disasters, or fighting against a powerful supervillain with a nefarious plan? Describe a typical day in the life of your superhero – how do they balance their superhero duties with their everyday life, and do they have a secret identity?

Think about what your character stands for and what lessons they teach. What lesson do they send about being brave, kind, and responsible? Finally, tell a story about an adventure where they saved the day. How do they use their abilities to get past problems or trick the bad guy? What effect do they have on the people they save and the area they keep safe?

Clarifying Questions:

1. How does your superhero handle the fame or anonymity that comes with being a hero?

2. What personal challenges or doubts do they face, and how do they overcome them?

3. If your superhero could team up with any other hero (real or fictional), who would it be and why?

Optional Activity:
Draw a comic strip or a poster featuring your superhero. Include scenes of them in action, using their powers, and the villain or challenge they are facing.

CHAPTER 81

MYSTERY AT THE MUSEUM

Prompt:
You find a mysterious object in a museum. Write a story about its history
and how you discovered its secret.

To Get You Started:

I MAGINE VISITING A MUSEUM and coming across an object that immediately piques your interest. It might be tucked away in a less-visited corner, partially hidden behind other exhibits, or perhaps it stands out because of its unusual appearance. Describe this object – is it an ancient artifact, a mysterious painting, an intricate mechanical device, or something else entirely? As you examine it, you feel there's more to its story than meets the eye.

Begin to unravel the mystery of this object. Maybe you find a hidden compartment, a cryptic inscription, or discover that it's connected to a legendary story or an unsolved historical mystery. Consider how you go about uncovering its secrets. Do you research its history, consult experts, or follow a series of clues that lead you on a journey of discovery?

As the story unfolds, dive into the history of the object. Who made it, what was its purpose, and how did it end up in the museum? Share the adventures, challenges, and surprises you encounter as you delve deeper into its past. Perhaps the object is linked to a historical figure, a forgotten civilization, or even extraterrestrial origins.

Finally, reveal the secret of the object. What significant discovery do you make, and how does it change your understanding of history, the object itself, or even your own life? Think about the impact of this discovery – does it solve a long-standing mystery, reveal a hidden truth, or lead to more questions?

Clarifying Questions:

1. How do you feel when you first encounter the mysterious object, and how do your feelings evolve throughout the story?

2. What skills or knowledge do you use to uncover the secret of the object?

3. If you could keep one memory from this adventure, what would it be?

Optional Activity:

Create a diary entry or a mini-exhibit display for the mysterious object, including a description, sketches or photos, and the story of how you uncovered its secret.

CHAPTER 82

THE LOST TREASURE MAP

Prompt:
You find an old treasure map. Describe your quest to find the treasure.

To Get You Started:

I MAGINE STUMBLING UPON AN old, weathered map, perhaps hidden in an attic, inside an old book, or washed up on a beach. The map is filled with cryptic symbols, mysterious landmarks, and a big 'X' marking a treasure's location. Describe how you feel when you discover the map and your decision to embark on a quest to find the treasure.

Think about the preparations you make for this adventure. What supplies do you gather, and who, if anyone, do you choose to bring along? Describe the journey as you follow the map. Maybe it leads you through dense jungles, across vast deserts, over treacherous mountains, or to a remote island. Consider the obstacles and challenges you encounter along the way. These could include deciphering clues, solving riddles, navigating through dangerous terrain, or even dealing with rivals also searching for the treasure.

As you get closer to the treasure, the anticipation builds. What do you find at the 'X' mark? Is it a chest of gold and jewels, a historical artifact, a family heirloom, or something entirely unexpected? Reflect on the journey's climax and the treasure's significance. How does finding the treasure (or the journey itself) change you? What lessons do you learn about adventure, friendship, and the value of the quest itself?

Clarifying Questions:

1. What is the most memorable moment of your treasure hunt?

2. How do the people you bring on your quest contribute to the adventure?

3. If you could embark on another treasure hunt, what would you do differently?

Optional Activity:

Draw the treasure map, including key landmarks and challenges you encountered. Next to it, sketch the treasure and write a short description of its significance.

CHAPTER 83

THE JOURNEY ON A GIANT BIRD

Prompt:
You befriend a giant bird and go on a journey. Where do you go and what do you see?

To Get You Started:

I MAGINE ENCOUNTERING A MAGNIFICENT, giant bird, perhaps an eagle, a phoenix, or a mythical creature, with wings that span wider than any bird you've ever seen. Describe your first interaction with this majestic bird and how you form a bond of friendship. What does the bird look like – what are its colors, and how does it communicate with you?

Think about the incredible journey you embark on with this giant bird. Where do you decide to go? Maybe you soar high above the clouds, exploring distant lands, hovering over snow-capped mountains, vast deserts, or lush rainforests. Describe the sights you see from this unique vantage point in the sky. What landmarks, natural wonders, or hidden places do you discover?

Consider the adventures and encounters you have along the way. Perhaps you witness a migration of animals from above, help other creatures in need, or find a hidden paradise that can only be reached by air. What challenges do you face during the journey, and how do you and the giant bird work together to overcome them?

Reflect on the bond you share with the bird and the perspective this journey gives you on the world. How does experiencing the world from the sky change your views or feelings about nature, freedom, and exploration?

Clarifying Questions:

1. What is the most breathtaking sight you see on your journey?

2. How do you communicate and collaborate with the giant bird during your adventures?

3. If you could take another journey with the giant bird, where would you go next?

Optional Activity:

Draw a series of scenes or a map charting your journey with the giant bird. Highlight key moments, discoveries, and the landscapes you see from above.

CHAPTER 84

THE HAUNTED HOUSE MYSTERY

Prompt:
You and your friends explore a haunted house. What mysteries do you solve?

To Get You Started:

I MAGINE YOU AND YOUR friends daring each other to explore an old, ru-
mored-to-be-haunted house in your neighborhood. Describe the house – is it an
ancient mansion, a dilapidated Victorian home, or an eerie abandoned cabin? As you step
inside, what do you feel and see? Maybe the air is cold, the floors creak with every step,
and portraits on the walls seem to watch you.

Think about the mysteries and legends surrounding the house. Perhaps there are tales
of hidden treasures, unsolved disappearances, or ghostly apparitions. What clues do you
find as you explore? You might come across an old diary, secret passages, hidden compartments, or mysterious symbols etched into the walls.

Consider the supernatural or eerie experiences you encounter. Do doors slam shut on
their own, are there unexplained whispers, or do shadows move in the corners of your
eyes? How do you and your friends react and work together to uncover the truth?

As you delve deeper into the mystery, reveal what you discover. Is there a logical expla-
nation for the strange occurrences, like hidden mechanisms or natural phenomena, or do
you uncover something truly supernatural? Reflect on the history of the house and the
resolution of its mysteries. What do you learn about bravery, friendship, and the power
of curiosity?

Clarifying Questions:

1. What is the most surprising thing you uncover in the haunted house?

2. How does solving the mystery change your perception of the house and its
   legends?

3. If you had the chance to explore another mysterious place, would you do it?

Optional Activity:

Create a map of the haunted house, including all the rooms, secret passages, and key places where you found clues. Illustrate and annotate the map with the discoveries and experiences you had in each location.

CHAPTER 85

THE SECRET LIFE OF A SPY KID

Prompt:
You're a kid spy on a secret mission. What gadgets do you use and what mystery do you solve?

To Get You Started:

I MAGINE YOURSELF AS A kid spy, equipped with an array of cool gadgets and on a mission to solve a perplexing mystery. Begin by describing your secret identity and the gadgets at your disposal. Do you have a watch that doubles as a communicator, shoes with hidden compartments, or sunglasses that can see through walls? Maybe you have a pen that's also a grappling hook or a notebook that turns into a tablet with access to any database.

Next, outline the mission you're tasked with. Is it uncovering a plot at your school, finding a lost invention, or maybe unmasking a secret villain in your neighborhood? Describe how you use your gadgets and wits to gather clues and follow leads.

Consider the challenges you face on your mission. Are there puzzles you need to solve, traps you have to avoid, or other spies you encounter? How do you use your gadgets creatively to overcome these obstacles?

As you get closer to solving the mystery, build up the suspense and excitement. What surprises or twists do you encounter? How do your observations and clever thinking help you crack the case?

Finally, reveal the resolution of your mission. What is the secret behind the mystery, and how do you bring a successful conclusion to your adventure? Reflect on what you've learned from this experience about bravery, intelligence, and the importance of being resourceful.

Clarifying Questions:

1. What is the most useful gadget in your spy toolkit, and why?

2. How do you balance your spy life with your everyday kid life?

3. If you could choose another kid to join your spy team, who would it be and what skills would they bring?

Optional Activity:

Draw a comic strip or a series of illustrations depicting a key scene from your spy mission. Include your gadgets in action and the crucial moment when you solve the mystery.

CHAPTER 86

THE VOLCANO ADVENTURE

Prompt:
You go on an expedition to an active volcano. What do you discover?

To Get You Started:

I MAGINE EMBARKING ON AN adventurous expedition to explore an active volcano. Describe your preparations for this daring journey – what equipment do you take, and who accompanies you? Maybe you have a geologist to help understand the volcanic activity, or a guide who knows the terrain.

As you approach the volcano, depict the changing landscape. Are there fields of hardened lava, steam vents releasing plumes of gas, or ash-covered trees? Describe the sights, sounds, and smells as you get closer to the volcano's crater. Is there a rumbling from deep within the earth, the hiss of escaping steam, or the sulfuric scent of volcanic gases?

Think about the discoveries you make during your expedition. Perhaps you find rare mineral formations, evidence of ancient eruptions, or unique plant and animal life adapted to the volcanic environment. Consider any challenges or dangers you face, like navigating rugged terrain, dealing with unexpected eruptions, or monitoring changes in volcanic activity.

Reflect on the climax of your adventure – reaching the rim of the volcano's crater. What do you see inside the crater, and how do you feel being so close to such powerful natural forces? Also, ponder the scientific and personal insights gained from this experience. What do you learn about volcanoes, the Earth's geology, and the thrill of exploration?

Clarifying Questions:

1. What is the most unexpected thing you learn or see on your volcanic expedition?

2. How do you ensure safety during your adventure near an active volcano?

3. If you could share one piece of information about volcanoes with others, what would it be?

Optional Activity:

Create a journal entry or a series of drawings documenting your volcanic expedition.

Include sketches of the landscapes, geological features, and any exciting moments or discoveries.

CHAPTER 87

THE SECRET DOOR

Prompt:

You find a secret door in your house. Where does it lead and what do you
find?

To Get You Started:

I MAGINE DISCOVERING A HIDDEN door in your house that you've never noticed before. It could be behind a bookshelf, under a staircase, or in a forgotten corner of the attic. Describe your initial feelings – are you surprised, curious, or a little bit scared? Think about what prompts you to open the door. Is it a sense of adventure, a family legend, or simply accidental discovery?

As you open the secret door, consider where it leads. Does it take you to a hidden room filled with old family heirlooms, a tunnel that goes deep underground, or perhaps a portal to another world or time? Explore the environment you find yourself in. What do you see, hear, and smell? Maybe there are ancient artifacts, mysterious writings on the walls, or a landscape vastly different from your own world.

Think about the discoveries and adventures you have after stepping through the door. Do you uncover family secrets, find a treasure map, meet a character from the past, or encounter magical creatures? Consider the challenges or puzzles you face in this hidden place. How do you navigate and interact with this new environment?

Reflect on how this discovery changes you. What lessons do you learn about bravery, curiosity, and the unknown? How does this secret door and the world it leads to affect your understanding of your home and your place in the world?

Clarifying Questions:

1. What is the most surprising or valuable thing you find through the secret door?

2. How do you keep the secret of the door, or do you decide to share it with someone else?

3. If you could choose a destination for the secret door to lead to, where would it be?

Optional Activity:
Draw a picture or a series of sketches showing what lies behind the secret door. Include captions or a brief story describing your journey and discoveries.

CHAPTER 88

THE NIGHT AT THE MUSEUM

Prompt:
Spend a night in a museum where exhibits come to life. What happens?

To Get You Started:

I MAGINE SPENDING A NIGHT in a museum where, as the lights dim and the moon rises, the exhibits begin to come to life. Describe the museum setting – is it a natural history museum with dinosaur skeletons and animal displays, an art museum with paintings and sculptures, or a science and technology museum with inventions and models?

As the museum transforms, narrate your initial reaction. Are you startled, amazed, or thrilled? Think about the first exhibit that comes to life and your interaction with it. Maybe a T-Rex skeleton roars to life, a famous figure in a painting steps out of their frame, or a historic spaceship invites you on a cosmic journey.

Explore the adventures that unfold during the night. Do you have conversations with historical figures, learn about ancient civilizations from the artifacts themselves, or get caught up in a battle between medieval knights? Consider the unique perspectives and stories each exhibit shares. What new insights do you gain into history, art, or science?

Reflect on the challenges or humorous situations you face. Perhaps you help a lost mummy find its way, play hide and seek with a group of paintings, or solve a puzzle with the help of a famous scientist.

As dawn approaches and the museum returns to normal, think about how this extraordinary experience changes your perception of the museum. What lessons do you learn about the magic of history and the power of imagination?

Clarifying Questions:

1. What is the most surprising or enlightening conversation you have with an exhibit?

2. How do you navigate the museum and keep up with the lively exhibits?

3. If you could bring one of the museum's exhibits to life in the real world, which one would it be?

Optional Activity:

Create a scrapbook page or a series of drawings depicting your night in the museum. Include captions describing your interactions with the exhibits and how they came to life.

CHAPTER 89

ALIEN FRIEND

Prompt:
An alien lands in your backyard and you become friends. What happens
next?

To Get You Started:

I MAGINE YOUR SURPRISE WHEN a spaceship lands in your backyard, and an alien emerges! Describe your first encounter. Is the alien tall or short, colorful or transparent, resembling something familiar or completely unlike anything on Earth? Despite the initial shock, you and the alien quickly become friends. What is the alien's name, and how do you communicate with each other?

Explore the adventures you have with your new alien friend. Maybe the alien shows you technology from their world, like a device that lets you experience different planets' environments or a gadget that creates holographic images. Think about the fun activities you do together. Do you show the alien around your town, introduce them to Earth's customs and foods, or maybe even have a space adventure?

Consider the challenges you face. How do you keep your new friend a secret, or do you decide to introduce them to your family and friends? What misunderstandings or funny situations arise from the cultural differences between you and your alien friend?

Reflect on what you learn from each other. What insights does the alien give you about the universe, life on other planets, and different perspectives? Similarly, what does the alien learn from you about life on Earth, human emotions, and our way of living?

Clarifying Questions:

1. What is the most surprising thing you learn about the alien and their culture?

2. How do your family and friends react if they meet the alien?

3. If you could visit the alien's home planet, what would you hope to see or learn?

Optional Activity:

Create a photo album or a series of drawings depicting memorable moments with your alien friend. Include captions describing each scene and the story behind it.

CHAPTER 90

A WORLD WITHOUT GRAVITY

Prompt:
Write about a day in a world where gravity doesn't exist.

To Get You Started:

I MAGINE WAKING UP TO find that gravity no longer exists. Describe your initial reaction and the peculiar sensations of floating freely in your room. How do you move around, and what adjustments do you make to perform simple tasks like eating, getting dressed, or reading a book?

Explore how the lack of gravity affects your daily routine. Do you tie yourself to furniture to avoid floating away, use fans or propulsion devices to move around, or create a system of ropes and pulleys to navigate your home? Think about the fun and playful activities you can do in a zero-gravity environment, like flying with a gentle push, performing acrobatic maneuvers, or playing sports in entirely new ways.

Consider how your community and the world adapt to this new reality. How do people travel, work, or go to school without gravity? Maybe public transportation includes floating buses, offices are equipped with anchoring systems, or schools hold classes in enclosed spaces where students and teachers float together.

Reflect on the challenges and advantages of a gravity-free world. Are there new inventions or methods developed to cope with everyday tasks? How does this change affect people's lifestyles, health, or the way they interact with each other?

As the day ends, ponder the implications of living in a world without gravity. What lessons do you learn about adapting to change and the importance of the forces that normally ground us?

Clarifying Questions:

1. What is the most enjoyable part of a gravity-free day, and why?

2. How do you overcome the difficulties or inconveniences of having no gravity?

3. If gravity returned, what aspect of the zero-gravity experience would you miss the most?

Optional Activity:

Draw a series of scenes depicting various activities in a world without gravity – from floating breakfasts to airborne commutes and zero-gravity sports.

CHAPTER 91

ROBOT BEST FRIEND

Prompt:

Write about your adventures with a robot best friend. What makes them special?

To Get You Started:

I MAGINE HAVING A ROBOT as your best friend. Describe what your robot friend looks like – are they humanoid, more like a classic robot, or something entirely unique? What features or capabilities do they have? Maybe your robot friend can change shapes, has a vast knowledge database, or possesses super strength.

Explore the special bond you share with your robot friend. What makes them your best friend? Is it their unwavering loyalty, their ability to always make you laugh, or the adventures you share? Think about the fun activities and adventures you experience together. Perhaps you go on a treasure hunt using the robot's scanning abilities, solve mysteries with their analytical skills, or simply enjoy playing video games with an unbeatable opponent.

Consider the challenges you face together. Maybe there are times when your robot friend needs repairs or must adapt to human emotions and social norms. How do you help each other grow and learn?

Reflect on the unique aspects of having a robot as a best friend. What lessons do you learn about friendship, technology, and the blending of the human and digital worlds? How does this friendship change your perspective on robots and artificial intelligence?

Clarifying Questions:

1. What is the most memorable adventure you have with your robot friend?

2. How do you communicate and understand each other, considering the differences between a human and a robot?

3. If you could upgrade your robot friend with a new feature, what would it be and why?

Optional Activity:
Draw a comic strip or a series of illustrations showing a typical day or a special adventure with your robot best friend. Include dialogue and captions to capture the essence of your friendship.

CHAPTER 92

A VISIT TO THE MOON

Prompt:
Describe a family trip to the moon. What do you see and do there?

To Get You Started:

IMAGINE your family embarking on an extraordinary trip to the moon. Begin with the excitement and preparations for this lunar adventure. What does your spacecraft look like, and how does your family react as you blast off into space?

As you journey to the moon, describe the experience of traveling through space. What do you see through the windows of your spacecraft – the Earth shrinking in the distance, the stars, other planets, or maybe passing satellites?

Upon landing on the moon, narrate your first steps on the lunar surface. How does it feel to walk in low gravity, and what do you see around you? Maybe you explore famous sites like the Sea of Tranquility or the Apollo landing areas. Think about the activities you do on the moon. Do you take a moon rover ride, collect moon rocks, or set up a family flag?

Consider the unique experiences of spending time on the moon. What games or fun activities can you do in low gravity, and how do you capture these moments? Perhaps you play lunar sports, take breathtaking photos, or have a picnic with space food.

Reflect on the sights of the lunar landscape – the vast craters, mountains, and the view of Earth from the moon. What feelings do these sights evoke in you and your family? How does this trip change your perspective on space, Earth, and the universe?

As your visit comes to an end, think about your journey back to Earth. What stories and memories do you bring back with you?

Clarifying Questions:

1. What is the most surprising or awe-inspiring thing you discover on the moon?

2. How do you and your family entertain yourselves during the trip to and from the moon?

3. If you could bring back one thing from the moon, what would it be?

Optional Activity:

Create a travel diary or a photo album of your family's trip to the moon. Include drawings or photos of key moments, and write descriptions or stories about your experiences.

CHAPTER 93

LIVING IN A VIDEO GAME

Prompt:

Suddenly, you find yourself inside your favorite video game. Describe your journey.

To Get You Started:

I MAGINE THE SURPRISE AND thrill of finding yourself inside the world of your favorite video game. Describe the moment you realize you've become part of the game. What does the game world look like? Is it a fantastical land filled with magic, a futuristic city with advanced technology, or a treacherous landscape with unknown dangers?

As you start your journey in the game world, think about your role. Are you the hero on a quest, a character with a special mission, or a regular inhabitant of the game world? Consider the abilities or powers you have – do you have super strength, magical powers, or advanced tech gadgets?

Explore the challenges and obstacles you face. Do you battle enemies, solve puzzles, or navigate through difficult terrains? Think about the allies you meet along the way – other characters who help you, offer advice, or join your quest. What friendships or alliances do you form?

Reflect on the missions or goals you must complete. Are you rescuing someone, searching for a treasure, or trying to save the game world from an impending threat? Describe the climactic moments of your journey – the battles you fight, the discoveries you make, and the decisions you take that impact the game's outcome.

As your adventure in the game world concludes, consider how this experience changes you. What lessons do you learn about courage, strategy, and teamwork? How does returning to the real world feel after your video game adventure?

Clarifying Questions:

1. What is the most exciting or challenging part of living in the video game?

2. How do you use your knowledge as a player to navigate the game world?

3. If you could bring one element or item from the video game into the real world, what would it be?

Optional Activity:

Draw a comic strip or a series of scenes depicting your adventure in the video game world. Include key moments, challenges, and allies or enemies you encounter.

CHAPTER 94

THE INVISIBLE CITY

Prompt:
There's a city that only appears once every hundred years. What happens
when you find it?

To Get You Started:

I MAGINE STUMBLING UPON A legendary city that materializes only once every hundred years. Describe your sense of wonder and disbelief as you witness the city appearing out of thin air. What does it look like? Is it a city of towering spires and grand buildings, a quaint village with ancient architecture, or a futuristic metropolis that seems out of place in time?

As you explore the city, consider the sights, sounds, and smells around you. Are the streets bustling with people from another era, or is it a ghost city waiting to be rediscovered? Think about the unique experiences and discoveries you make in this city. Maybe you find markets selling impossible wares, libraries with ancient wisdom, or gardens with otherworldly plants.

Ponder the mysteries and secrets of the city. Why does it appear only once every hundred years, and what hidden knowledge or treasures does it hold? Perhaps you meet inhabitants or guardians of the city who share its history and stories.

Reflect on the challenges you face during your visit. Are there puzzles to solve or riddles to answer to unlock the city's secrets? Consider what happens as the city begins to fade away. What do you take back with you – memories, a mysterious artifact, or a life-changing revelation?

Clarifying Questions:

1. What is the most fascinating aspect of the invisible city that captivates you?

2. How does the experience of being in the city change your perspective on history or the flow of time?

3. If you could bring someone with you to the city, who would it be and why?

Optional Activity:

Draw a map or a series of sketches of the invisible city, highlighting key locations, encounters, and discoveries you make during your exploration.

CHAPTER 95

THE FLOATING ISLANDS

Prompt:
Describe a world where islands float in the sky. How do people travel and live there?

To Get You Started:

I MAGINE A WORLD WHERE instead of being anchored in the sea, islands float amidst the clouds in the sky. Begin by describing the appearance of these floating islands. Are they small and numerous like a scattered archipelago, or are there a few large, sprawling islands? What features do they have – lush greenery, waterfalls cascading into the clouds, or unique wildlife?

Consider how people have adapted to living on these floating islands. What kind of houses do they build – do they have structures anchored to the ground, or do they live in homes suspended in the air? Think about the daily life and culture of the islanders. What do they eat, how do they gather resources, and what kind of traditions or festivals might they have in a world among the clouds?

Explore the methods of transportation both within and between the islands. Do people travel using airships, hot air balloons, or even domesticated flying creatures? Maybe there are bridges of clouds or ropes, or a system of pulleys and platforms for moving from one island to another.

Reflect on the adventures and challenges of living in a world of floating islands. Are there islands that are still unexplored, mysterious weather phenomena, or rare, valuable resources to be discovered? What kind of trades or occupations are unique to this skyward world?

Clarifying Questions:

1. What is the most breathtaking view or natural wonder you find on one of the floating islands?

2. How do the islanders interact with any visitors from the ground below?

3. If you could choose an island to live on, what features would it have?

Optional Activity:

Draw a picture or a series of sketches depicting life on the floating islands. Include details like housing, transportation methods, and the daily activities of the islanders.

CHAPTER 96

THE PET CLOUD

Prompt:
You have a cloud as a pet. What fun activities do you do together?

To Get You Started:

I MAGINE HAVING A CLOUD as your unique and magical pet. Describe what your pet cloud looks like – is it fluffy and white, constantly shifting shapes, or does it have a shimmer of colors like a sunset? Think about how you care for your cloud pet. Does it need to be kept in open spaces, how do you feed it, and what keeps it happy?

Explore the fun activities and adventures you have with your pet cloud. Perhaps you go on sky-high rides, floating above your town or soaring among the stars at night. Consider the playful things your cloud can do – maybe it can change shapes at your request, create gentle rain to water plants, or provide shade on a sunny day.

Reflect on the unique bond you share with your cloud. Does it have a personality, how does it communicate its emotions, and what special moments do you share? Think about the challenges of having a cloud as a pet. How do you keep it from floating away, or what do you do when the weather changes?

Contemplate the lessons and insights gained from having a cloud as a pet. What do you learn about the sky, weather, and the environment? How does this special friendship change your perspective on nature and the world around you?

Clarifying Questions:

1. What is your favorite activity to do with your cloud pet, and why?

2. How do others react to seeing your unique pet, and how do you explain its nature?

3. If you could go on one grand adventure with your cloud, where would you go and what would you do?

Optional Activity:
Draw a series of pictures showing different activities and adventures with your pet cloud. Include captions describing each scene and the fun you have together.

CHAPTER 97

THE REVERSE WORLD

"THE REVERSE WORLD"

Prompt:

You enter a world where everything works in reverse. How is your day different?

To Get You Started:

I MAGINE STEPPING INTO A world where all the rules are flipped and everything operates in reverse. Describe your initial reactions to this topsy-turvy world. What are the first things you notice that are different? Maybe the sun rises in the west and sets in the east, people walk backward, or water flows upward.

Think about how a typical day unfolds in this reverse world. What happens at mealtimes – do you start with dessert and end with appetizers? Consider how communication works; perhaps conversations start with goodbye and end with hello. Reflect on the activities of daily life, like reading books from back to front or playing sports where the objective is to lose instead of win.

Explore the unique challenges and humorous situations you encounter. How do you adapt to walking backward, and what is it like to see cars driving in reverse on the streets? How do people in this world use technology or go about their jobs in a reverse manner?

Contemplate the interactions you have with the inhabitants of the reverse world. What insights do they share about living life in reverse, and what new perspectives do you gain? How does this experience change your understanding of time, causality, and the way we perceive normalcy?

As your day in the reverse world comes to an end, reflect on what you've learned. How does this adventure influence your thoughts about your own world and the way things are done?

Clarifying Questions:

1. What is the most challenging part of adapting to the reverse world?

2. How do your habits and behaviors change during your time in this world?

3. If you could bring one aspect of the reverse world back to your normal life, what would it be?

Optional Activity:

Draw a comic strip or a series of scenes depicting your experiences in the reverse world. Highlight the differences in daily activities, interactions, and the world's unusual aspects.

CHAPTER 98

THE FRIENDLY ALIEN VISIT

Prompt:
A group of friendly aliens visit your school. What do you show them
about Earth?

To Get You Started:

I MAGINE THE EXCITEMENT AND curiosity when a group of friendly aliens unexpectedly visits your school. Start by describing the aliens – what do they look like, how do they communicate, and what is their spaceship like?

Think about what you would want to show these extraterrestrial visitors about Earth and human culture. Perhaps you start with a tour of your school, explaining the different subjects and activities students participate in. Show them a typical classroom, the library, the playground, and the cafeteria. How do the aliens react to the books, games, and school routines?

Consider what aspects of Earth's culture you'd want to share. Maybe you introduce them to music, art, and sports. You could show them how to play a musical instrument, draw a picture, or participate in a simple game. Think about the foods you'd want them to try. What would be on the menu for an alien-friendly school lunch?

Reflect on the questions the aliens might have about Earth. What do they find most interesting or surprising about human life? Are they curious about our planet's environment, history, or technology?

As the visit comes to an end, think about what message you want to leave with the aliens about Earth and humanity. What do you hope they remember most about their visit, and what do you learn from them about their own world and culture?

Clarifying Questions:

1. What is the most surprising question the aliens ask about Earth or humans?

2. How do you and your classmates communicate with the aliens if they speak a different language?

3. If you could visit the aliens' planet, what would you be most interested in seeing or learning?

Optional Activity:
Create a photo album or a scrapbook page documenting the aliens' visit to your school.

Include drawings or photos of the activities and interactions, along with captions describing the experiences.

CHAPTER 99

THE JOURNEY TO A PARALLEL UNIVERSE

Prompt:
You find a portal to a parallel universe. What is different there and what
adventures do you have?

To Get You Started:

I MAGINE DISCOVERING A MYSTERIOUS portal that leads to a parallel universe. Describe your initial reaction and the moment you decide to step through the portal. What does the journey through the portal feel like, and what do you see and experience as you transition to another universe?

As you emerge in the parallel universe, observe the differences from your world. Is it a mirror image of your world with subtle changes, or is it vastly different, with unique landscapes, architecture, and technology? Maybe the laws of physics are altered, or the society has a different cultural or historical development.

Explore the adventures you have in this parallel world. Do you meet alternate versions of people you know, encounter new species, or discover advanced technologies or magic? Think about the challenges you face in navigating this new world. Are there language barriers, unfamiliar customs, or unknown dangers?

Reflect on the lessons and insights you gain from your journey. How does this experience change your perspective on your own world and your place within it? Consider the relationships you form and the impact of your actions in this parallel universe.

As you return to your world, ponder the connections between the two universes. What do you bring back with you – knowledge, memories, or a new understanding of the possibilities of existence?

Clarifying Questions:

1. What is the most surprising difference you find in the parallel universe?

2. How do you adapt to the rules and customs of the parallel world?

3. If you could bring one element from the parallel universe back to your world, what would it be?

Optional Activity:

Create a travel diary or a series of postcards from the parallel universe. Include descriptions and drawings of the places, people, or phenomena you encounter on your adventure.

CHAPTER 100

THE PLANET OF CANDY

Prompt:
You land on a planet where everything is made of candy. Describe your
sweet discoveries.

To Get You Started:

I MAGINE THE EXCITEMENT OF landing on a planet entirely made of candy. As you step out of your spacecraft, describe the landscape that greets you. Is the ground a soft sponge cake, are the mountains giant scoops of ice cream, or do rivers of chocolate and soda flow through the land?

Explore the various regions of this candy planet. Maybe you wander through forests where the trees are made of licorice and cotton candy, climb jelly bean hills, or relax on beaches where the sand is fine sugar. What unique and delicious flora and fauna do you encounter? Perhaps there are gummy bear creatures roaming around, lollipop flowers blooming, or marshmallow clouds floating in the sky.

Think about the adventures you have on this sweet planet. Do you go on a quest to find the rarest candy, participate in a festival celebrating the planet's confectionery delights, or invent new candy combinations with the ingredients you find?

Reflect on the challenges you might face in a world made of candy. How do you ensure you have a balanced diet, and how do you handle the sticky, melty, or hard surfaces? What solutions do you come up with to navigate and live in this sugary environment?

As your journey on the candy planet comes to an end, consider what you take back with you to Earth. What knowledge, experiences, or actual sweets do you bring back as souvenirs?

Clarifying Questions:

1. What is your favorite candy discovery on the planet, and why?

2. How does the experience of being on a candy planet affect your appreciation for sweets?

3. If you could share one aspect of the candy planet with people on Earth, what would it be?

Optional Activity:

Create a travel brochure or a series of postcards for the candy planet. Include illustrations of the landscapes, the candy creatures, and the adventures you have, along with descriptions of each scene.

CHAPTER 101

THE WEATHER CONTROLLER

Prompt:
You can control the weather with a special device. What do you do with this power?

To Get You Started:

I MAGINE YOU HAVE A device that gives you the ability to control the weather. Describe the device – is it a remote control, a smartphone app, or something more mysterious like a magical amulet or a futuristic gadget?

Think about the first time you use the device. What weather do you create, and why? Maybe you bring rain to a drought-stricken area, create a sunny day for a community event, or gently coax snow to fall softly in your neighborhood. Consider the reactions of those around you and the impact of your weather choices on the environment and people's lives.

Explore the responsibilities and challenges that come with such a power. How do you decide when and where to change the weather? Are there ethical considerations, like impacting natural weather patterns or choosing one location's needs over another? Reflect on how you balance personal desires with the greater good.

Consider the adventures and unexpected situations you encounter. Perhaps you accidentally trigger a storm and have to fix it, or you're asked to help with a major event or crisis by controlling the weather. How do you handle these scenarios?

As you become more experienced with the weather controller, think about the lessons you learn about nature, science, and the consequences of human intervention. How does this power change your perspective on the environment and your role in the world?

Clarifying Questions:

1. What is the most challenging decision you face regarding weather control?

2. How do you feel about the power to control weather, and how do you handle the responsibility?

3. If you could permanently change one aspect of your local weather, what would it be?

Optional Activity:

Draw a comic strip or a series of scenes showing how you use the weather controller. Include the effects of your weather changes and the reactions of people and animals.

ALSO BY JEFFREY C. CHAPMAN

Adulting Hard for Young Men

Adulting Hard for Young Women

Adulting Hard After College

Adulting Hard in Your Late Twenties and Thirties

Adulting Hard For Couples

Adulting Hard for New Parents

Adulting Hard as an Introvert or Highly Sensitive Person

Adulting Hard and Laughing Harder

Adulting Hard: Life Skills for Teens

101 Self-Care Activities

Made in United States
Orlando, FL
26 September 2024

51991464R00124